THE ENCYCLOPEDIA OF PROPHECY

D1532366

BOOKS BY OMAR V. GARRISON

Tantra
Spy Government
The Dictocrats
Howard Hughes in Las Vegas
Lost Gems of Secret Knowledge
Balboa: Conquistador
The Hidden Story of Scientology
The Secret World of Interpol

According to many commentators, the final Antichrist will at
first present himself in the guise of the new Messiah. (The word
Antichrist means "instead of Christ" as well as "against Christ".)
"The Reign of Antichrist depicted above is after an engraving
by Michael Volgemuth in the *Liber Chroniclorum, 1493.*

THE

ENCYCLOPEDIA

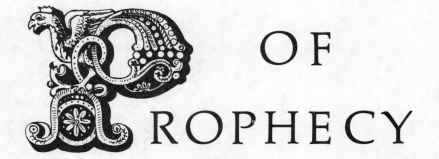

OF

ROPHECY

By

Omar V. Garrison

CITADEL PRESS • SECAUCUS, N.J.

First paperbound printing, 1979
ISBN 0-8065-0674-1

Published by Citadel Press
A division of Lyle Stuart Inc.
120 Enterprise Ave., Secaucus, N.J. 07094
In Canada: George J. McLeod Limited, Toronto
Manufactured in the United States of America

INTRODUCTION

PROPHECY IS AS OLD AS THE HUMAN RACE.
Faced with the uncertainty, if not the menace, of the future, people of every age and place on earth have tried to penetrate the barrier of time that separates us from tomorrow's world.

The need to know what lies ahead becomes especially acute in periods of great cultural and political upheavals. That is why, in our own day, we are witnessing an extraordinary revival of popular interest in prophecy. The global wars, the economic chaos, the rapidly changing social standards; above all, the spreading fear that in our lifetimes all will end in a vast nuclear holocaust, have stimulated new interest in the predictions of great seers, past and present.

What have these visionaries, who claim to foretell the course of Providence, to tell us? How trustworthy are their revelations and by what criteria can their accuracy be judged? Does the remarkable agreement which links the prophecies of all ages mean that they are true? Or that, as the Swiss psychiatrist Jung theorizes, they merely represent something called archetypal constellations in the unconscious mind?

In order to answer such questions, it is necessary to take a fresh look at the words and forecasts of those prophets, famous and obscure, whose voices have been raised in exhortation and warning over the centuries.

This book is intended to serve that purpose. In the following pages will be found, in reference form, the principal themes of prophecy throughout the ages, as well as a brief look at the personalities behind them.

These can here be viewed both from the perspective of history and from the vantage ground of contemporary events.

If only a fraction of what the prophets have told us is true, the importance of such a review cannot be overestimated. For perhaps the first time in human history, the future of mankind truly hangs in the balance. Even the immediate years ahead are of vital concern in most people's lives. The reason is that we are being swept along by a torrential tide of change that is moving with a greater speed than man has ever experienced before. If there is one point on which both secular forecasters and inspired mystics agree, it is that during the brief two and a half decades separating us from the year 2000, the present world order will undergo a total change.

But what kind of change? The various answers to that question bring into sharp focus the difference between the inspired prophet, who claims a supernatural origin for his revelations, and the scientific futurist, who bases his predictions on extrapolation—that is, projecting known facts into the future.

It has been only recently that some orthodox scientists have acknowledged that foreseeing the future is, in fact, possible. Studies conducted by reputable researchers within the university setting have led a few advanced thinkers cautiously to admit the existence of two kinds of knowledge: the scientific-intellectual and the mystic-intuitional.

"These two ways of thinking," wrote the famous physicist, Robert Oppenheimer, "the way of time and history, and the way of eternity and timelessness, are both part of man's effort to comprehend the world in which he lives. Neither is comprehended in the other nor reducible to it, each supplementing the other, neither telling the whole story."[1]

As for foreseeing the distant future, the mystics have a better record for accuracy than have the rationalists. Perhaps one reason for this is that scientific prediction, like all scientific methods, is logical, while the course of human history is illogical. It is full of surprises, unexpected turns, amazing discoveries, catastrophic intrusions by natural phenomena, and so on.

In short, the future is not, for the most part, within easy reach of *factual* conjecture.

When it comes to foreseeing what lies ahead, even that overpraised non-human oracle, the "electronic brain" or computer, is no match for an uncomplicated Washington real-estate broker named Jeane Dixon, or a simple, untutored photographer called Edgar Cayce.

Rationalists, of course, will not agree with that assertion. They point out that seers, who derive their knowledge from esoteric sources, do not provide definite, intelligible information about the future. They are usually vague in their statements and when their predictions can be understood, more often than not miss the mark.

All of which is true. Yet, if we examine the record,

[1] Quoted in the anthology, *The Nature of Human Consciousness*, edited by Robert E. Ornstein. N.Y., 1974.

we find instances in which inspired individuals have been accurate in describing—sometimes in amazing detail—future events which scientists at the same time were declaring to be impossible.

For example, in 1856 (when the automobile was still a half century in the future, and the aeroplane even more remote), the American prophet Andrew Jackson Davis clearly foresaw both. Predicting that there would be "a great improvement in motive forces," he wrote:

> "Carriages will be moved by a strange and beautiful and simple admixture of aqueous and atmospheric gases—easily condensed, so simply ignited, and so imparted by a machine resembling our [steam] engines, as to be entirely concealed and manageable between the forward wheels."

This superior motive power, he went on, would also make possible aerial navigation, so that "aerial cars also will move through the sky from country to country; and their beautiful influence will produce a universal brotherhood of acquaintance."[2]

It is enlightening to compare this remarkable prophecy with the utterances of leading scientists who right up to the time of the Wright brothers were insisting that heavier-than-air machines would never fly.

Typical of the dominant opinion of that time was the flat statement by Simon Newcomb, a prominent mathematician-astronomer. He declared:

"No possible combination of known forms of machinery and known forms of force, can be united in a practical machine by which men shall fly long distances through the air."

It is true that Davis in his vision saw only the "beau-

[2] Andrew Jackson Davis, *The Penetralia*. New York, 1856.

tiful influence" of the airplane flying from country to country. But a century earlier, one of his predecessors, assuming the more traditional role of the prophet—that of forewarning as well as foretelling—supplied the darker side of the picture. In 1760, the English visionary Thomas Gray wrote: "There will come a time when thou shalt lift thine eyes/To watch a long-drawn battle in the skies;/ While aged peasants, too amazed for words/stare at the flying feet of wondrous birds."

What was the source of this amazing foreknowledge? How could a mystic poet in the 1700's describe a scene which was to take place over a century and a half later and for which there was not at that time anything even remotely related to it?

The prophets themselves have said that what they perceive comes to them unsought and from another world which exists either outside of time, or one in which events, past present and future, all exist simultaneously.

For this reason it is very difficult for them to pinpoint an exact date on which their predictions will be fulfilled.

Those who have attempted to do so have misdated events by anything from a month to a millenium.

Religious prophets have traditionally dated their predictions by "signs of the times" given in the Bible. This has proved to be a very unreliable method, owing to the ambiguity of the Scriptural text. St. Paul says, for instance, that God will intervene directly to terminate human history when evil has reached its climax. But to every generation, that point in man's history seems to have been reached.

The result has been countless end-of-the-world scares, starting as far back as A.D. 534 and continuing periodically down to the present.

Apparently, the biggest panic of the kind occurred toward the end of the last millenium. Throughout Europe, great numbers of people, misinterpreting Biblical prophecy, were convinced that the Day of Judgment, prophesied in the Apocalypse, was at hand. It was widely preached and believed that Christ would make his promised reappearance in Jerusalem.

Mackay, author of the minor classic, *Popular Delusions and Madness of Crowds*, has given us a vivid description of the scene. He writes that in the year 999, the vast number of people streaming toward the Holy Land was so great they were compared to a desolating army. Before leaving Europe, they sold all their possessions to finance their pilgrimage and sojourn in Jerusalem while awaiting the second Advent. "Buildings of every sort were suffered to fall into ruins. It was thought useless to repair them, when the end of the world was so near. Many noble edifices were deliberately pulled down. Even churches, so well maintained, shared the general neglect. Knights, citizens and serfs, travelled eastward in company, taking with them their wives and children, singing psalms as they went, and looking with fearful eyes upon the sky, which they expected each minute to open, to let the Son of God descend in his glory."

Even though the faith of these legions of the hopeful ended in disillusionment, and for many, poverty, the same mistake on a smaller scale, was repeated again in 1100, 1200, and 1245.

In fact, the millenarian idea has, down the centuries, exerted a powerful influence over those Christians who "search the scriptures" for clues to the final consummation of history. Past errors in date-setting have not discouraged true believers.

Are the supernaturally inspired prophets of all ages wrong, then, in their insistence that the consummation of the centuries must inevitably come? Was St. Malachy indulging in a flight of Irish fantasy when, in the

11th century, he listed every successive pontiff to occupy the chair of Peter, from Celestine II (1143–1144) onward to the final Peter of Rome, designating each by a Latin motto and indicating that only three more popes will follow the present Paul VI, before the end of the world? Will many of us live to witness the great earthquakes, tidal waves and reversal of the earth's poles, as foretold by Nostradamus, Cayce and others—all associated with the time of the end?

A great many fundamentalist Christians see in the current Middle East imbroglio fulfillment of Biblical prophecy. They point out that their long-standing prediction—often laughed at—of an "ingathering of the Jews" to their homeland has come true. Likewise, their prophetic belief that the Jews would reoccupy the Temple site in Jerusalem, last held by them in A.D. 70, was vindicated when Israeli forces took the Old City in 1967. The next important development on "God's timetable," according to these interpreters of divine revelation, will be the destruction of the Moslem mosque now on the site, to be followed by the rebuilding of the Third Temple. When it is completed, the Son of Perdition or Antichrist will appear, initiating the final seven years of human history. During the last three and a half years of that period, an all-obliterating war will devastate the planet, followed by the return of Jesus and a thousand years of utopian bliss.

The evangelicals see in the technological developments of our day instruments for the fulfillment of prophecy. For example, in a book, *Satan In The Sanctuary*, after noting that in the past commentators were hard put to explain to believers just how everyone in the world could witness the return of Jesus at the same time, as promised in Revelation 1:7: "Behold, he is coming with the clouds; and every eye shall see him," the authors write:

"An intriguing possibility, hitched again to our modern times and our concept of things, is satellite television. The image of Christ would indeed be beamed on the clouds, and accessible to every eye at once."[3]

Even if we do not share the apocalyptic vision of the fundamentalists, most of us have the vague feeling that we are moving toward a major crisis. Events of the last two decades have not been reassuring.

Let us take a realistic view of the world today: our continued existence hangs by a thread. We face the imminent possibility of what Dr. Henry A. Murray of Harvard termed "an utterly disgraceful end to man's experience on earth." Nations large and small are stockpiling weapons of mass destruction on a scale never known before. So far, no way has been found to control this insane rush toward annihilation of the human race.

The terrible finale could come when mortal error, inspired by fear, presses the fatal button to release a nuclear war that will eventually engulf the world. Even as I write these lines, the sinister long missiles are poised deep in their silos; are carried by aircraft endlessly circling the skies; and are nestled aboard submarines gliding silently beneath the seas, year in and year out.

Or, think about this: Herman Kahn, former luminary of the famous Rand Corporation in Santa Monica, California, not long ago published results of a study he made for the U. S. government at a cost of 73 million dollars. It was the analysis of a cobalt superbomb which, with curious irony, he called the Last Judgment. Its destructive power would be sufficient to annihilate all life on this planet. Attached to the monster weapon would be a computer which would record all atomic

[3] Thomas S. McCall and Zola Levitt, *Satan in the Sanctuary*. Chicago, 1973.

explosions on earth and when radioactivity had reached a given level, would activate the Final Judgment.

Kahn's colleagues in the advanced analysis field hastened to express total skepticism concerning the material published in his report. Still, it demonstrates some of the high-level thinking in certain areas of government. It is doubtful that even the big spenders in Washington would have squandered 73 million dollars on a work of science fiction.

For the oracles of systematic knowledge, then, the future is being *made* in the scientific laboratories and advanced technology centers of the world's industrialized nations. For the soul-inspired prophets, it is being *fulfilled* in such historical events as the sudden rise of Arab power (predicted by Nostradamus, Joachim of Floris and others); establishment of the European Common Market; and the disintegration of the Roman Catholic Church. (Regarding the latter phenomenon, Dr. Malachi Martin, a Jesuit scholar, recently predicted: "Well before the year 2000 there will no longer be an institution recognizable as the Roman and Apostolic Church of today!")

Even when the futurists are optimistic about human survival, come what may, the picture they paint for us is that of a strangely alien world, filled with prodigies and wonders: human colonies on Mars; cities on and under the sea; living brains without bodies; people whose behavior is remotely controlled by electrodes implanted in the brain; contact with beings from other planets.

With respect to future encounters between earthlings and beings from other worlds, a Russian scientist and Nobel prizewinner, Nikolai Semionov, even foresees the bizarre meeting of man with anti-man somewhere in space. He reminds us that our galaxy is composed of substances whose atoms have nuclei made up of protons and neutrons enclosed in an electron "wrapper," and points out the possibility that there are other galaxies whose substances are made up of just the opposite— that is, of anti-matter.

"In these other worlds," he writes, "we would find the same combination of chemicals, with the same structures and the same properties; and it is very possible that living matter and even human beings could exist in them. Let us imagine the meeting of a man and an anti-man in some part of outer space. They would be able to study each other and even become intimate friends, but they could never touch each other. If they tried to do so, both would explode with a force much greater than that of the thermonuclear bomb."[4]

Unlike the scientist, whose predictions, however fantastic, are thus highly-educated guesses rather than precognition, the religious seer has the added mission of exhorting us about coming events. His message has a profound moral purpose. It is intended to prepare us spiritually for a coming time of tribulation. We are told in frightening detail what we can expect, and warned that we must mend our ways if we hope to escape disaster. "He that taketh warning," declared the prophet Ezekiel, "shall deliver his soul."

By taking warning, then, can we *change* the future? Is tomorrow alterable by what we do today, or is it a ready-made reality awaiting us, horrors and all?

To date, the best answer to that question—from scientist and seer alike—is that in some things we have a freedom of choice, but not in others. As J. B. Priestley puts it, in his thought-provoking book, *Man and Time*, the future is already shaped, but still pliable.

That being so, the panorama of prophecy presented in the following pages could provide the coordinates needed to re-structure our destiny.

[4] Nikolai Semionov, *As I See The Future*. Paris, 1960.

ABOMINATION OF DESOLATION.   A curious expression, first occurring in the prophecies of Daniel. It is used to describe one of the events of "the last days" in which an evil power or person will occupy, pollute and make desolate the sanctuary of God.

Many commentators believe that the description refers to Antiochus Epiphanes and his setting up an altar to the Olympian Jove in the Temple at Jerusalem—a sacrilege that sparked the Maccabean revolt in 168 B.C.

However, Jesus used the same phrase (Matt. 24:15 and Mk. 13:14) to foretell an event that was to take place after his time on earth.

Many students of Biblical prophecy regard Daniel's statement as referring to Messianic times, that is, when the Antichrist profanes the tabernacle of the Third Temple in Jerusalem, yet to be built.

Some interpreters of the Nostradamus *Centuries* have advanced the theory that the abomination of desolation will come at the end of the present century.

ADAMS, MARSHAM. An eminent Oxford scholar and Egyptologist, who initiated studies of the Great Pyramid, which led to the development of several systems of messianic prophecy based upon interpretation of ancient Egyptian literature and monuments.

His theories are expounded in his principal work, entitled *The Book of the Master*.

ADSO (A.D. 954). The abbot of a medieval monastery in Moutier-en-Der, France, whose treatise, *De Antichristo*, describes events which will precede the end of the world. The work, which he dedicated to Queen Gerberge, tells of the struggle against the prophetic Antichrist, or Man of Sin, who will appear in the last days to seduce men with his Satanic powers, but who will ultimately be overthrown. He wrote:

> "The Antichrist will launch a terrible persecution of people throughout the world. He will use three kinds of weapons: terror, gifts, and miracles. This fearful tribulation will last three and a half years —the forty-two months of the Apocalypse."

AIELLO, SISTER ELENA (b. 1919). An Italian nun and visionary, most of whose prophecies warn of future disasters such as epidemics, famine, earthquakes, etc., that await humanity because of its corruption and materialism.

> "Great calamities will be seen in the world," she wrote in 1959, "bringing confusion, tears and sadness for all. Great earthquakes will submerge [coastal] cities. Epidemics and famine will play great havoc, especially where the sons of darkness are to be found. Never has the world in this tragic hour more need of prayer and pentitence."

Sister Elena, who vainly warned Mussolini at the outbreak of World War II that Italy would suffer disaster
and defeat if he allied himself with Hitler, has predicted
that "Russia will march on Europe, and especially on
Italy, with much ruin and desolation." The Soviet flag,
she said, will fly on the cupola of St. Peter's in Rome.

Her revelations, which she said came to her from the
Blessed Virgin, all urge repentance and rejection of the
extreme corruption into which the entire world has
fallen:

> "The anger of God is at hand and the world will be
> struck by great calamity . . . The world will be
> convulsed in a new and terrible war! Deadly
> armies will destroy nations, peoples, and all the
> things they love. In this profane struggle, much
> that has been made by the hand of man will be
> destroyed. The dictators of the earth—truly in-
> fernal monsters—will raze the churches with their
> Sacred Food. Clouds bright with fire will suddenly
> appear across the sky and a storm of fire will beat
> down on all the world. This terrible scourge,
> never before seen in human history, will last for
> seventy hours. The recusant will be reduced to
> powder, and many will be lost in the obstinacy of
> their sins. Then the power of light will be seen
> above the power of darkness."

The nun's final prophecy, given in August 1960, once
again repeated the warnings sounded in her previous
messages to the world. She predicted that "Russia, with
its secret armies, will fight America, conquer Europe,
and the river Rhine in Germany especially will be seen
full of corpses."

ALPHA AND OMEGA.   Alpha and Omega, the first
and last letters of the Greek alphabet, are used in the

Apocalypse (q.v.) to express the idea of God's eternity and the fulfillment of prophecy. "I am Alpha and Omega, the beginning and the ending, saith the Lord, which is, and which was, and which is to come, the Almighty." (Rev. 1:8)

The symbol was derived from an earlier Hebrew tradition in which the first and last letters of the Hebrew alphabet—Aleph and Thaw—form the initial and terminal letters of the word *Emeth* meaning truth. For Jewish mystics the term embodied the notion of perfection and completion, the prime attributes of Jehovah. Aleph, the first letter of *Emeth*, signifies that God was the beginning; *thaw*, the final letter, that He is also the end and consummation of all things. Thus, the word Emeth or Truth was known as "the seal of God."

AMERICA IN PROPHECY.   The United States has figured in a surprisingly small number of major prophecies, considering the country's major role in world affairs. Even among those forecasts which do include America, either by name or by inference, there is more than the normal amount of contradiction.

The scientific futurists appear to have taken a greater interest in the future of America than have the inspired prophets. The extrapolations of these academic savants are mostly concerned with such aspects of the nation's future as population growth, sex ratio, economic curves, achievements in science, environmental conditions, racial relationships and, of course, the overriding if not overwhelming problem of nuclear war.

The futurists do not usually make hard and fast predictions. They merely say what *might* happen or, at most, what *probably* will occur, projecting their forecasts in a straight line from present conditions.

An example of this kind of prophetic relativity is Herman Kahn's study of what he calls "the Armageddon situation," which he defines as "a final battle between 'good' and 'evil' in which civilization itself will receive an enormous setback no matter who wins the battle or, even more finally, a battle in which human life will be wiped out."

Kahn points out that this possibility will not always be just an academic notion. Only some satisfactory form of world arms control could prevent such a doomsday, but he is pessimistic about the ability of the U.S. to cope with the problem vis-à-vis the Soviet Union. His rational look into the future seems to come close to paralleling that of the mystics.

Kahn implies that the Soviet leaders are manipulating American fears of Armageddon for their own advantage. He warns that "it is dangerous to put tempting strategies before an opponent."

> "Our emphasis clearly must be on balanced and achievable goals," he writes in *On Thermonuclear War*, "and on means appropriate to them. Thus we must stress objective military capabilities, genuine arms controls agreements, and international arrangements which are not a disguised form of unilateral surrender. This will involve some hard bargaining and risky tactics, but barring some unforeseen good or bad luck, this seems to be the only practical approach—*competent military preparations plus tough-minded but genuine bargaining*. There is doubt in my mind whether the West can measure up to the demands of the situation."

Viewing the future of America thus as one fraught with grave risks and uncertainty, Kahn seeks to explain the danger in terms of human shortcomings rather than divine retribution for sin.

"If the history of the decline of the West has to be written in the year 1980," he says, "it is likely to be occasioned by: (1) the nation's tendency to hold excessively firm positions in a crisis; (2) increasingly widespread ignorance of the technical side of war; and (3) crises that tend to induce excessive physical and mental strain in crucial individuals."

Kahn predicts that if the Russians keep their capabilities secret and increase or change their program, "it is likely we will not react adequately—even if we get moderately good intelligence. Barring a crisis, our country is very loath to spend money on military goods. I make this statement fully aware that we are currently budgeting a great deal of money . . . for national security."

In his long look at American destiny, Kahn fully takes into account the x-factor, that irrationality of history which the inspired prophets view as the hand of God:

"The uncertainties and risks of the future are increased by the mounting race of technological progress. It is not at all unlikely that there may be some invention or discovery which cannot be handled even momentarily in our present international society. Progress is so fast, the problems are so unprecedented, and the lead times for cultural assimilation so long, that it is difficult to believe that we will understand our system well enough to prevent accidents, miscalculations, or the need for dangerous improvisation in a crisis or unexpected contingency."

While America, representing the forefront of scientific and technological advances, looms large in the prognostications of futurists, it figures in only a few of the oracles based on divine revelation.

Some students of Biblical prophecy have tried to read America directly into their exegeses, but they have found the task a demanding one. The Judeo-Christian scriptures, which have provided the broad basis for most current previews of the world's future, have little or nothing to say specifically about the U.S.A., as they appear to do about Israel, Russia, Europe and countries of the Middle East.

Count Louis Hamon, better known as Cheiro, solved the problem of bringing America into the mainstream of Biblical prophecy by relating its destiny to that of Israel. In 1925, he wrote:

> "The 'fadic' or important dates of the United States appear to coincide so mysteriously with those concerning the past history of the Israelites and the promise of their return to their own land that it forces one to come to the conclusion that the United States will in the near future play a most important role in the opening up and development of Palestine. 'The Precession of the Equinoxes' which I have alluded to before, giving periods of time that average 2150 years, fits in with the destiny of the United States as they have done with the history of the Israelites. This mysterious period of years is considered by many students of such things to foreshadow the length of time known as 'The Times of the Gentiles' when Jerusalem would be 'trodden under foot,' and the many prophecies that when this time would be fulfilled the Israelites would return to power must, to my mind, be fulfilled just as other prophecies concerning this race have been fulfilled in the past. The difficulty being solely to establish when

'the Times of the Gentiles' commenced, for if this
could be once and for all definitely settled the rest
would be only a matter of simple calculation."

The overall picture of America that emerges from the
various predictions of contemporary seers is one of decline in prestige and power in the world; of natural
calamities, a racial war, a continuing masculinization of
women; the emergence of a despotic and powerful cen-
tralized government; and moral decadence.

There are a few dissenting voices—prophets who en-
vision a spiritual regeneration and restoration of the
country's moral leadership of the world, but they are in
the minority.

Alan Vaughan, an American sensitive who works as
a researcher in the parapsychology field, has set down
these prophecies regarding the future of the United
States, based, he says, on the archetype of Roman
civilization:

— The American president will acquire greater and
  greater power.

— The Senate and the House of Representatives will
  correspondingly lose power, being demoted to the
  status of yes-men.

— The government will become increasingly corrupt
  and resort to devious methods to maintain control.

— Semimilitary organizations at the capital (like the
  Roman Praetorian Guard) will increase in power such
  that eventually they will control the presidency.

— Eastern culture will heavily influence American
  thought in years to come. Eastern cults and religions
  will gain strength here and finally supplant traditional Christianity. A new religion will combine Eastern and Christian concepts.

— Americans will become less concerned with individual freedom and more concerned with security. Guaranteed incomes and even more lavish television spectaculars will correspond to "bread and circuses."

— America's technology will rise to new heights.

— Armies will shrink in size, Americans will no longer be drafted (already a virtual certainty). Foreign nationals will be employed in peace-keeping operations.

— America will become more and more dependent on importing goods from other countries.

— The percentage of affluent Americans will continue to grow, as will their decadent excesses. Yet an influential minority will continue to fight to maintain older standards.

— A clash with the "barbarians" (probably Russians) will weaken America but put it into alliance with Russia. In fact, the clash may already have happened, being dubbed the Cold War, the Korean Police Action, and Vietnam. The alliance with the Soviet Union should follow soon, but with America in a weaker position than now.

— *A Pax Americana*—a period of relative lack of war—should be soon upon us. Optimism should run high, decadence should run wild, and the stage will be set for America to begin a search for new spiritual values.

Another contemporary American seer and clairvoyant, Daniel Logan, has also made a number of predictions concerning important future events affecting the destiny of the United States. In trance readings, he has foreseen the destruction of New York, and cataclysmic earth changes as envisioned by Edgar Cayce; radical alteration of climate in most of the country; and a major war between the U.S. and China in the late 1980's.

During one of his trance sessions, a "spirit entity," speaking through Logan also foretold the end of the presidency in America:

> "The 1980s will see the last of your presidents in office. The responsibility will be taken from the president and given to several men; at least five will be in the position that one man is in today. This allocation of duty will work far better than placing all the responsibilities—and thus draining all the energies of one man."

ANTICHRIST.   The name given the mysterious "man of sin" or "son of perdition" whose appearance in the world, according to Biblical prophecy, will immediately precede the second advent of Jesus Christ.

Scriptural as well as secular prophets describe him as the ancient adversary of mankind, who will embody everything diabolical, cruel and deceptive. His brief but terrible reign over the earth will be marked by bloody wars, persecutions and universal suffering.

The first mention of the name Antichrist occurs in the Epistles of John, in the New Testament; but the idea has its roots in the Old Testament, especially in the prophecy of Daniel, in which is prefigured the evil adversary of God.

The final Antichrist, who will appear at the end of time, will have many forerunners. The first of these was no doubt Antiochus Epiphanes, whose character and personality traits are in a general way duplicated by his historical successors.

According to many commentators, the final Antichrist will at first present himself in the guise of a new Messiah. (The word antichrist means "instead of

Christ" as well as "against Christ"). As the Satan counterfeit of the true Christ, he will have the power to perform wonders and to attract a worldwide following. He will persecute and put to death all who refuse to pay him homage, or who continue in their practice of rival faiths.

Jeane Dixon, a Washington matron who has become well known as a seeress, pictures the Man of Sin as a sinister politico-military figure. She suggests that many, if not all, his "miracles" will be technical or scientific achievements. He will hold out the prospect of universal affluence, "liberation" from the "bondage" of past ideologies and religious beliefs; and will bring about world peace.

> "The Antichrist will be a phenomenon of the po-
> litical order," she writes. "He is not simply a re-
> ligious heretic whom the world at large could
> simply ignore. He will hold earthly power in his
> hands and use it as his instrument. All the tyrants
> of history are mere children in comparison with
> him.
> "This means first of all that he will be a military
> figure beyond anything the world has previously
> seen. He will conquer the whole earth and hold it
> in complete mastery with the most modern weap-
> ons. He will rule his new World Empire with the
> utmost military might and glory . . . He will es-
> tablish and lead a strange and fundamentally
> anti-human 'religion' of atheism and anti-re-
> ligion."

Individual nations will disappear, says Mrs. Dixon, and "the whole world will become an island in the universe." Thus, the world government, so ardently sought by many factions today, will come about, but it will be a terrifying despotism which will extend into the life of every individual, controlling even their thoughts.

The Antichrist will employ the American media as an indispensable means of spreading his doctrines.

Gongenot des Mousseaux, a 19th-century French commentator, also viewed the future Antichrist as a political figure so far as his public image is concerned. "He will be, to all appearances, a great revolutionary, who will bow to no authority other than his own will."

Mousseaux also envisioned him as the supreme commander of a global army, who will mercilessly exterminate all who resist him. The followers of Christ will experience wholesale persecution greater than any known since the first-century pogroms of Nero and Caligula.

Prophetic writers of ancient times (as well as a few recent ones) have said that the Antichrist will be the offspring of a human mother and a demon, or even Satan himself.

Hildegarde, the 11th-century mystic, for example, declared that "after having spent a licentious youth in the company of dissolute men, the mother of the Son of Perdition will be carried to a deserted place by a demon. There she will conceive and give birth [to the Antichrist] without knowing the father's identity."

The prophecy of La Salette (q.v.) makes a somewhat similar prediction. According to that version, the Antichrist will be born of a nun "who will have intimate relations with the ancient serpent."

Because of his diabolical origin, Hildegarde continues (in Vision X, Part III), "nothing good will enter into him nor be able to be in him. For he will be nourished in diverse and secret places, lest he should be known by men, and he will be imbued with all diabolical arts, and he will be hidden until he is of full age, nor will he show the perversities which will be in him, until he knows himself to be full and superabundant in all iniquities.

"But from the beginning of his course many battles and many things contrary to the lawful dispensation will arise, and charity will be extinguished in men. In them also will arise bitterness and harshness, and there will be so many heresies that heretics shall preach their errors openly and certainly: and there shall be so much doubt and incertitude in the Catholic faith of Christians that men shall be in doubt what God they invoke, and many signs shall appear in the sun and moon, and in the stars and in the waters, and in other elements and creatures, so that, as it were in a picture, future evils shall be foretold in their portents.

"Then also so much sadness shall occupy men at that time, that they shall be led to die as if for nothing. But those who are perfect in the Catholic faith will await in great contrition what God wills to ordain. And these tribulations shall proceed in this way, while the son of perdition shall open his mouth in the contrary doctrine. But when he shall have brought forth the words of falsehood and his deceptions, heaven and earth shall tremble together. But after the fall of Antichrist the glory of the Son of God shall be increased.

"As soon as he is born, he will have teeth and pronounce blasphemies; in short, he will be a born devil. He will emit fearful cries, work miracles, and wallow in luxury and vice. He will have brothers who are also demons incarnate, and at the age of twelve, they will distinguish themselves in brilliant achievements. They will command an armed force, which will be supported by the infernal legions."

A contemporary writer, whose study of Biblical

prophecy is based on Fundamentalist interpretation, describes the Antichrist as a "Great Dictator" or "The Future Fuehrer."

> "His conquest will be rapid," wrote Hal Lindsey in *The Late Great Planet Earth.* "He will be very strong and powerful, and there will be an air about him which is self-assured and proud.
> "The way in which this dictator is going to step onto the stage of history will be dramatic. Overnight he will become the byword of the world. He is going to be distinguished as supernatural; this will be done by an act which will be a Satanic counterfeit of the resurrection. This writer does not believe it will be an actual resurrection, but it will be a situation in which this person has a mortal wound. Before he has actually lost his life, however, he will be brought back from the critical wounded state. This is something which will cause tremendous amazement throughout the world."

Lindsey, in common with those of his persuasion (whose beliefs are derived mainly from the Book of Revelation in the New Testament and the Book of Daniel in the Old Testament), asserts that the Antichrist will be a spellbinding orator, who will offer peace to a world that wants more than anything else, freedom from war. They will increasingly pledge their allegiance to the Great Dictator who promises the end of all conflict.

In support of this conclusion, Lindsey cites not only the Scripture, but also the eminent British historian, Arnold Toynbee: "We are ripe for the deifying of any new Caesar who might succeed in giving the world unity and peace."

This means world government, the groundwork of

which has already been laid in the United Nations.

There is general agreement among almost all visionaries who have foretold the coming of the Man of Sin that his birth will occur "in the last days" of earth. However, the dates given for his advent have varied considerably.

As early as the fifteenth century, Vincent Ferrer, a Dominican monk and celebrated seer of Valencia, Spain, wrote Pope Benedict XII that he knew for certain that the Antichrist was already nine years of age and would make his public appearance in a few years.

Again in 1613, a Dominican friar named Sebastian Michalies declared that revelations made to him by exorcised demons indicated that the Antichrist was three years old at that date. "He was baptized on the Witches' Sabbath in the presence of his mother, a Jewess called Belle-Fleur. Louis Gaufridi is said to have baptized him in a field near Paris."

Gaufridi was the French priest who, after being tortured, was burned at the stake in 1611 as a sorcerer.

At the beginning of the present century, Pope Pius X who, in a vision, foresaw the Vatican overrun by Communists, believed that the Antichrist of Christian prophecy was already at work in atheistic Western society. He wrote that "such a spiritual perversion is the beginning of the evil announced for the end of time, and the Son of Perdition which is mentioned by the Apostles is here among us now."

Vladimir Soloviev, the noted Russian philosopher and mystic, predicted that the final Antichrist would be born in 1954.

Innocent Rissant, an interpreter of the Nostradamus prophecies, linked the Antichrist's birth to the appearance of a comet in the skies above Rome in the year of Pope Pius XII's death—that is, in 1963.

However, Jeane Dixon pinpoints the birth date of the

Son of Perdition as being precisely February 5, 1962 at 7 A.M. She wrote that "the circumstances of his birth, and the events that I have seen, makes his life very much like that of Christ; nevertheless so different that I have never had any doubt at all that this child will be no other than the Antichrist who could deceive the world . . ."

Mrs. Dixon identifies the sinister child's birthplace as somewhere in the Middle East, and implies that he may be a direct descendant of the ancient Egyptian Pharaoh Ikhnaton and his wife, Nefertiti.

The Washington seeress described a remarkable vision she had of the "Child of the East" wrapped in swaddling clothes in imitation of the infant Jesus, held in the arms of his mother, Queen Nefertiti, who symbolically presented him to the world.

Mrs. Dixon said that following his birth the child's parents took him to another country of the Middle East, where "there are forces working around him, which are protecting him. The possibility exists that the child and his parents may again move to another country."

Meanwhile, as he was nearing the age of twelve years (1974), the young Antichrist would become aware of his Satanic mission.

> "He will then expand his influence, and those around him will finally form a small nucleus of dedicated followers when he reaches the age of nineteen. He will work quietly with them until he is twenty-nine or thirty years old, when the forcefulness and impact of his presence in the world will begin to bear his forbidden fruit.
> "In the same manner as Christ and his disciples spread the Gospel, so the child and his disciples will propagate the religion of the false god. The difference will be, however, that they will not

stand alone, but will have the power and the propaganda machine of the United States backing them, advancing his cause beyond anything ever thought possible."

As the global influence of the Antichrist and his followers grows, the prestige of Christianity will wane. By the time the Antichrist is thirty years of age (i.e., 1990), Christian education of youth will have reached a standstill, making them highly receptive to the blandishments of the new gospel.

> "I see that the youth of the world will accept him and will walk closely with him in placing the world into his eager hands . . . No one will be able to hold the children back, for to capture the youth, and through them the world, the little boy was born."

Still paralleling the life of Jesus, the work of the Antichrist will be based in Jerusalem, although his field of operation will be the entire planet. "Close cooperation between the then ruling powers in the United States and the new 'spiritual' ruler will expose Americans to him in person, as his visits here will be frequent."

According to various prophecies (all faithful to the Book of Revelation), the formal reign of the Antichrist, established by bloodshed and deceit, and sustained by terror, will last three and a half years. "And there was given to him a mouth speaking great things and blasphemies; and power was given unto him to continue forty and two months." (Rev. 13:5)

Even though three and a half years appears to be a rather brief period in the world's history, even for such absolute power and so imperious a ruler as the Antichrist, the terror and devastation of the world during that time will be out of all proportion to its short span.

In fact, Jesus himself, referring to that interval of great tribulation "such as has not occurred since the beginning of the world," declared that "except those days should be shortened, there should no flesh be saved." (Matt. 24:21)

The end will come for the Antichrist when Jesus appears and annihilates him "with the breath of his mouth" and "with the brightness of his coming." (II Thess. 2:8)

Hildegarde, the 12th-century German mystic, in her book of prophecy describes the final act thus:

> "After the Son of Perdition has carried out all his evil designs, he will call together all his followers and tell them that he wishes to ascend into heaven.
> "In the moment of that ascension, a lightning flash will strike him, killing him.
> "The mountain from which he had planned to make his ascension will at once be covered with a dense cloud from which will issue a dreadful and truly infernal odor of corruption."

APOCALYPSE.   A writing which reveals future events; especially the prophetic literature of the Old and New Testaments. The word is derived from the Greek *apokalypsis*, meaning discovery or unveiling.

The best-known and most widely studied apocalypse is the final book of the New Testament, called the *Book of Revelation* in the Protestant version, and the *Apocalypse* in the Catholic. Sir Isaac Newton once said of it: "To explain this book perfectly, is not the work of one man or of one age; but probably it never will be understood till it is all fulfilled."

There is some difference of opinion among scholars regarding the authorship of the Apocalypse, although historically, it has been attributed to John the Apostle. That was certainly the view of the earliest commentators on the subject, among them Clement of Alexandria (c. A.D 200), Tertullian (c. 200), Athanasius (c. 293–373), Cyril of Alexandria (376–444), and Gregory of Nyssa (c. 331–396).

Even those modern authorities who have expressed doubts concerning the apostolic authorship of the Apocalypse agree that it was written by an early Christian prophet named John, who occupied a place of high respect among the Christian congregation in Ephesus.

On balance, the evidence seems to favor those who claim that the work was indeed the writing of John, the beloved disciple of Jesus, and that it was composed sometime during the reign of the Roman emperor Domitian (81–96) on the Greek island of Patmos.

John's revelations embody two divisions—one a brief prophecy for his own time and the other his principal message, an apocalypse of the last days, describing the final conflict between good and evil, to be resolved by the triumphant return of Jesus Christ.

The prophetic disclosures are presented in a series of visions, which unfold in symbolic form, foreshadowing the terrible events of the last days.

John says that he beheld a door opened in heaven and heard a voice speaking to him like a trumpet. It told him, "Come up hither, and I will show thee the things which must be hereafter."

The prophet was then transported in spirit into heaven where he saw in God's right hand a scroll sealed with seven seals. Until this time, no one in heaven or earth has been found worthy to open and read the contents of the scroll. But now Jesus appears and takes the scroll from God's hand. He begins to break the seals; as each is broken, cataclysmic events occur.

The opening of the first four seals release the famous

Four Horsemen who are, respectively, the white, representing a conqueror; the red, representing war; the black, famine; the sickly pale, pestilence "and his name that sat on him was Death," followed by Hell.

When Christ broke the fifth seal, John saw the martyrs who had been slaughtered on earth because they had borne testimony to God's word. Each of them was given a white robe, and they were told to rest a while longer until their fellow believers in Christ should be martyred as they had been.

The breaking of the sixth seal produces a violent earthquake. The sky turns as black as a funeral pall and the moon becomes blood-red. The stars of heaven fall to earth "even as a fig tree casteth her untimely figs, when she is shaken of a mighty wind." The sky vanishes like a scroll being rolled up, and every mountain and island on earth is moved from its place.

A half-hour of silence follows the breaking of the seventh seal. Then seven angels appear, each of whom is given a trumpet. The blowing of each trumpet heralds a new calamity upon earth. The first sound of the first trumpet produces hail and fire, mingled with blood, which consumes a third of the trees and all the grass on the planet. At the blast of the second trumpet, a huge mass "as it were a great mountain, burning with fire" is cast into the sea, the third part of which turns to blood. A third of all life in the sea perishes: and a third of all ships upon its surface are destroyed.

The sound of the third trumpet is followed by the fall from the sky of a great star, "burning as it were a lamp." It pollutes a third of the rivers and springs on earth, with the result that great numbers of people die from poisoned waters.

When the fourth trumpet is sounded, darkness covers a third part of sun, moon and stars. John sees an eagle flying through mid-heaven, calling with a loud cry,

"Woe, woe, woe to the inhabitants of the earth, when the trumpets sound which the three last angels must now blow."

The flourish of the fifth clarion opens the bottomless pit of hell to release a vast swarm of infernal locusts that have stings like scorpions. They do not attack vegetation, but for the space of five months they injure those people who have not received the mysterious "seal of God" in their foreheads. The tormented will seek death in their agony, but death will elude them.

John's description of the "locusts" in this passage suggests some kind of invading humanoids. The New English Bible translation of Chapter 9, verses 7 through 11 reads:

> "In appearance the locusts were like horses equipped for battle. On their heads were what looked like golden crowns; their faces were like human faces and their hair like women's hair; they had teeth like lion's teeth, and wore breastplates like iron; the sound of their wings was like the noise of horses and chariots rushing to battle; they had tails like scorpions, with stings in them, and in their tails lay their power to plague mankind for five months. They had for their king the angel of the abyss, whose name, in Hebrew, is Abaddon, and in Greek, Apollyon, or the Destroyer."

At the sound of the seventh trumpet, four angels are released from bondage to lead a vast army of 200 million men from the region of the Euphrates. They will kill a third of all mankind. The prophet says they had been held ready for this preordained moment—"for this very year and month, day and hour."

There follows in John's prophecy an interpolated vision in which he leaps ahead to the final days of earth, before resuming his account of the terrible catastrophes that are to be visited upon sinful mankind. In his intermediate revelation, John discusses various symbolic portents seen in the heavens and tells how the Archangel Michael and his angels wage a war against the dragon, "the serpent of old that led the whole world astray, whose name is Satan or the Devil." Satan and his forces are thrown down to earth, where they make war against "those who keep God's commandments and maintain their testimony to Jesus."

Two antichrists (called beasts in the revelation) appear to aid Satan in his bid to destroy the righteous and rule the world. One beast comes from the sea, and is described as resembling a leopard, but having feet like those of a bear and a mouth like that of a lion. The people of the world, says John (except those whose names are written in the book of life), will follow the beast in wondering admiration, chanting, "Who is like the Beast? Who can fight against it?" His reign over the earth will last forty-two months.

The second beast comes from the earth. It wields all the authority of the first beast, whom it compels the world's people to worship. It works miracles, "even making fire come down from heaven before men's eyes." It will require everyone—great and small, rich and poor, slave and free—to be branded with a mark on his right hand or forehead.

The first beast, or antichrist, then, will be a political figure; the second will be the founder of a new kind of religion, who will delude the people of earth and make them erect an image in honor of the first beast. (See article under *Antichrist*.)

Meanwhile, the faithful are seen gathered around Christ in security on a symbolical Mt. Zion. Three angels appear in turn to adjure mankind to fear God and to pay Him homage ("for the hour of His judgment has come"); to foreshadow the fall of Babylon the great (that is, Rome); and to warn that whoever worships the beast and receives its mark on his forehead or hand shall incur eternal damnation.

The final seven woes that are to plague the earth are symbolized in the outpouring of seven bowls "full of the wrath of God." These include such afflictions as malignant sores on the bodies of the Beast's followers; deep, painful sunburn; and unnatural darkness over the world. After the last bowl is emptied on the air, a voice says, "It is over!" and there are flashes of lightning and peals of thunder, followed by the most violent earthquake this planet has ever experienced. Cities of the world fall in ruins; and huge hailstones weighing as much as a hundred pounds fall from the sky.

Jesus appears, seated upon a white horse, and the two beasts which come out of the earth and sea are defeated in the final great battle. Their master, Satan, is cast into hell.

John's two closing chapters tell of a new heaven and a new earth—the heavenly Jerusalem—that will follow the horrendous events of the Last Judgment. The prophet hears a loud voice proclaim:

> "Now at last God has his dwelling among men! He will dwell among them and they shall be his people, and God himself will be with them. He will wipe every tear from their eyes; there shall be an end to death, and to mourning and weeping and pain; for the old order has passed away!"

ARABS IN PROPHECY. The almost overnight resurgence of the Arab bloc as a world power through the wealth and the economic influence of petroleum is the most startling phenomenon of the 20th century.

By a radical escalation of world oil prices, the cartel

countries at a single stroke concentrated much of the world's money reserves in their exchequers. What this would mean to the rest of mankind—and especially to the West—became a subject of much speculation.

> "In terms of international economics and politics," said John Emerson, leading economist for the Chase Manhattan Bank, "Middle Eastern oil is the world's balance wheel."

Students of Biblical prophecy say that this development was foreseen and foretold by the Old Testament prophets. Citing various passages in the books of Isaiah, Daniel and Ezekiel, interpreters of this school have predicted that the Arab countries will join with black African nations to form an alliance which was designated by biblical prophets as King of the South. The Arab-African confederacy will then unite with Soviet Russia (called King of the North) to attack the restored state of Israel, then under the governance of a false Messiah.

However, the invaders will be destroyed by some kind of supernatural intervention, which Israelis will openly acknowledge to be divine.

The *Centuries* of Nostradamus are also said to prefigure the evolution of a powerful Arab confederacy which, according to the prophet, will invade Europe:

> "The Great Camel (the Arab alliance) shall come to drink the waters of the Danube and the Rhine. The people of the Rhone shall tremble, and even more so, those of the Loire." (*Centuries* V:68)

Not even an approximate date is given for this event. Elsewhere in his prophecies, Nostradamus states that "through the discord and negligence of the French, a way will be opened for the Arab confederacy to invade Southern Europe through the harbour of Marseilles."

(I:18). Southern Spain will also be attacked, following the betrayal of that country by a Spaniard of Cordoba.

A number of 19th-century millenialists identify Mohammedan power as "the antichrist of the East." To most of these earlier exegesists, however, the Islamic power was understood to mean Turkish aggression.

ARMAGEDDON.   Literally, the mountain of Megiddo. It is the place, situated on the great plain of Jezreel at the foot of Mt. Carmel, where, according to Biblical prophecy, a final battle will be waged between the forces of good and evil, "the battle of the great day of God Almighty."

In the *Apocalypse* of John, Armageddon is mentioned (16:16) as the locale where the sixth bowl will be poured out: "And he gathered them together into a place called in the Hebrew tongue Armageddon."

Historically, a great many battles have already been fought in this area—notably that in which King Joshua received a mortal wound during the bloody fight with Necho, the Pharaoh of Egypt.

Later (Judges 5:19) Barak, the son of Abinoam, who was chosen to deliver the Hebrews from the bondage of the Canaanites, here defeated Sisera, general of King Jabin's powerful army.

Some contemporary expositors of Scriptural phophecy identify the great army of "the kings from the East" (Rev. 16:12) as one made up of the Chinese and their allies, who will march against the Western armies, led by a great monarch or dictator.

Descriptions of the carnage that will ensue when the opposing forces meet are mind-boggling. In the *Apocalypse*, John foresees a slaughter of millions. Characterizing the conflict as "the great winepress of the wrath of God," he prophesies that rivers of blood will rise to the height of the horses' bridles for a distance of 1,600 furlongs, which is equivalent to 200 miles.

ASTROLOGY.   Prophecy based upon the movement and influence of the stars and planets has been practiced for thousands of years.

In ancient Babylonia and Assyria, the priests employed astrology to divine future events as being the will of the gods who determine human fate.

From Babylonia, the study and practice of the "celestial art" passed into Greece, and through the Greeks was introduced into Egypt, India, and China. In Imperial Rome, for a time it held a high place as a reliable means of foretelling what would befall both the state and important individuals. Caesar Augustus (63 B.C.– A.D. 14) sought to discourage predictions based on astrological computations, and banished leading astrologers from Rome. Some of his successors, however, recalled them. Others—notably Vitelius and Domitian—were hostile to soothsayers of all kinds, and especially to practitioners of judicial astrology.

Despite this official disfavor, however, the art continued to flourish and was secretly patronized by influential public figures in Rome.

During the middle ages, the Arabs revived the star lore of the ancients, translating Ptolemy's work under the title of *Almagest*. The system was carried into Spain by the Moorish conquest, where it was further elaborated by both Jewish and Christian scholars.

One ancient Arabic prophecy predicts that the end of the present world order will occur at the time Jupiter and Saturn both enter the sign of Libra. The exact configuration is given as Saturn and Jupiter in conjunction at 9 degrees, 29 minutes in Libra—that is, on December 31, 1980.

Nostradamus, the greatest prophet of the Renaissance, if not of all time, based his famous predictions in part upon astrological calculations, at which he excelled. In his letter of dedication to his son, Nostradamus wrote:

> "Chiefly abhor the vanity of the execrable magic forbidden by the Sacred Scriptures and by the canons of the Church; except from this judicial astrology by which, and by means of divine inspiration, with continual calculations, we have put in writing our prophecies."

Contemporary seers who base their prophecies on astrology predict major political changes and realignments in international affairs when the world enters another solar cycle in 1981, initiating the pre-apocalyptic era.

ATLANTIS.   For centuries, the mystery of lost Atlantis, the island continent which, legend says, was swallowed up by the sea during a great cataclysm, has intrigued historians, archaeologists and mystics alike. Hundreds of books have been written on the subject since Plato first offered a brief history and description of the utopian land in two of his dialogues—*Timaeus* and *Critias.*

Students of prophecy are interested in Atlantis because of predictions by several seers that it will rise again from the depths of the sea during the present century.

Plato's account locates Atlantis "west of the Pillars of Hercules" (i.e., the Strait of Gibraltar). It was larger than North Africa and Asia Minor put together and encircled by a number of islands. By passing through these latter, one could reach the opposite continent, assumed by later writers to be America.

Atlantis, wrote Plato, "was the heart of a great and

wonderful empire, which had rule over the whole island and several others."

As the power and wealth of Atlantis grew, the Atlanteans extended their sovereignty beyond their islands and that part of the other continent which they had colonized, as far as Egypt and Tyrrhenia in Europe.

The Atlantean expansion was halted by the Athenians, who defeated them by superior military skill.

> "But afterward, there occurred earthquakes and floods, and in a single day and night . . . the island of Atlantis disappeared beneath the sea. And that is the reason the sea in those parts is impassable and impenetrable, because there is such a quantity of shallow mud in the way; and this was caused by the subsidence of the island."

All this happened about 9,000 years before Plato's time, or about 11,500 years ago.

In *Critias*, Plato describes Atlantis in detail as a land rich in natural abundance, whose cities had buildings of impressive architecture, lavishly adorned with gold, silver, ivory, brass, tin, and a mysterious metal called *orichalcum*, which glowed like fire.

> "Because of the greatness of their empire, many things were brought to them from foreign countries, and the island itself provided much of what was required by them for the uses of life. In the first place, they dug out of the earth whatever was to be found there, mineral as well as metal, and that which now is only a name and was then something more than a name, orichalcum, was dug out of the earth in many parts of the island, and with the exception of gold, was esteemed the most precious of metals among the men of those days. There was an abundance of wood for

carpenter's work, and sufficient maintenance for tame and wild animals.

"Moreover, there were a great number of elephants in the island, and there was provision for animals of every kind, both for those that live in lakes and marshes and rivers, and also for those which live in mountains and on plains; and therefore for the animal which is the largest and most voracious of them.

"Also, whatever fragrant things there are in the earth, whether roots, herbage, or woods, or distilling drops of flowers or fruits, grew and thrived in that land; and again, the cultivated fruit of the earth, both the dry edible fruit and other species of food, which we call by the general name of legumes, and the fruits having a hard rind, affording drinks and meats and ointments, and good store of chestnuts and the like, which may be used to play with, and are fruits which spoil with keeping, and the pleasant kinds of dessert which console us after dinner, when we are full and tired of eating—all these that sacred island lying beneath the sun, brought forth fair and wondrous in infinite abundance."

The principal city of Atlantis was circular in form, approximately fifteen miles in diameter. In the center of this large circle was an acropolis, set upon a hill. Surrounding the hill were alternate rings of land and water, connected by bridges. The main docks of the city were situated along the outermost ring of the metropolis's eastern side. Ships entered the vast circle through an enormous canal three hundred feet in width and a hundred feet in depth.

On the central island, the Atlanteans built a royal palace which "they continued to ornament in successive generations, every king surpassing the one who came before him to the utmost of his power, until they made the building a marvel to behold for size and for beauty."

They also erected on the center island a temple dedicated to Cleito and Poseidon, traditionally considered the progenitors of the race. The shrine was surrounded by an enclosure of gold. Here, too, was Poseidon's own temple, the exterior surface of which, with the exception of the pinnacles, was covered with silver. The pinnacles themselves were sheathed in gold.

Inside the temple, "the roof was of ivory, adorned everywhere with gold and silver and orichalcum; all other parts of the walls and pillars and floor, they lined with orichalcum."

"In the temple they placed statues of gold—there was the god himself, standing in a chariot—the charioteer of six winged horses—and of such a size that he touched the roof of the buildings with his head. Around him there were a hundred Nereids riding on dolphins, for such was thought to be the number of them in that day. There were also in the interior of the temple other images which had been dedicated by private individuals. And around the temple on the outside were placed statues of gold of all the ten kings and of their wives; and there were many other great offerings, both of kings and of private individuals, coming both from the city itself and from the foreign cities over which they held sway. There was an altar, too, which in size and workmanship corresponded to the rest of the work; and there were palaces in like manner, which answered to the greatness of the kingdom, and the glory of the temple.

"In the next place, they used fountains both of cold and hot springs. These were very abundant, and both kinds wonderfully adapted to use by reason of the sweetness and excellence of their waters. They constructed buildings about them and planted suitable trees; also cisterns, some open to the heaven, others which they roofed over, to be used in winter as warm baths. There were the king's baths, and the baths of private persons, which were kept apart; also separate baths for women, and others again for horses and cattle, and to each of them they gave as much adornment as was suitable for them. The water which ran off they carried, some to the grove of Poseidon, where were growing all manner of trees of wonderful height and beauty, owing to the excellence of the soil; the remainder was conveyed by aqueducts which passed over the bridges to the outer circles. There were many temples built and dedicated to many gods; also gardens and places of exercise, some for men and some set aside for horses, in both of the two islands formed by the zones; and in the center of the larger of the two there was a race-course of a stadium in width, and in length, allowed to extend all around the island, for horses to race in. Also, there were guard houses at intervals for the body-guard, the more trusted of whom had their duties appointed to them in the lesser zone, which was nearer the Acropolis; while the most trusted of all had houses given to them within the citadel, and about the persons of the kings.

"The docks were full of triremes and naval stores, and all things were quite ready for use.

"Enough of the plan of the royal palace. Crossing the outer harbors, which were three in number, you would come to a wall which began at the sea and went all around: this was everywhere distant fifty stadia from the largest zone and harbor, and enclosed the whole, meeting at the mouth of the channel towards the sea. The entire area was densely crowded with habitations. The canal and the largest of the harbors were full of vessels and merchants coming from all parts, who, from their numbers, kept up a multitudinous sound of human voices and din of all sorts night and day."

In concluding this account, Plato, as well as many of the writers on Atlantis who followed him, attributed the downfall of the lost kingdom to its moral decline. In their arrogance and power, the Atlanteans lost control of themselves and, while they did not have the insight to recognize the evil of their society, God "who has the gift of sight," saw all too clearly their degraded state. Plato says that they were guilty of disgracefully abusing their souls, the divinest part of man. What happened to them was not an act of justice, but of retribution. They perished in order that the rest of the world might be saved.

Plato's words have an ominously contemporary ring:

"For many generations—as long as the divine nature lasted in them—they were obedient to the laws, and well-affectioned towards the gods, who were their kinsmen; for they possessed true and in every way, great spirits, practising gentleness and wisdom in the various chances of life, and in their intercourse with one another. They despised everything but virtue, not caring for their present state of life, and thinking lightly of the possession of gold and other property, which seemed only a burden to them; neither were they intoxicated by luxury; nor did wealth deprive them of their self-control; but they were sober and saw clearly that all these goods are increased by virtuous friendship with one another, and that by excessive zeal for them, and honor of them, the good of them is lost and friendship perishes with them.

"By such reflections and by continuance in them of a divine nature, all that which we have described waxed and increased in them; but when this divine portion began to fade away in them and became diluted too often and with too much of the mortal admixture, and the human nature got the upper hand, then they, being unable to bear their fortune, became unseemly, and to him who had an eye to see, they began to appear base and had lost the fairest of their precious gifts; but for those who had no eye to discern the true happiness, they still appeared glorious and blessed at the very time when they were filled with lawless ambition and power.

Recent excavations, made under the direction of Greek archaeologist Spyridon Marinatos, on the Aegean island of Santorini have uncovered frescoes, artifacts, and architectural remains that closely resemble Plato's description. These finds have led some scholars to believe that the island was, in fact, the legendary Atlantis.

Santorini, also known as Thera, is the remaining part of what was a larger land mass which literally exploded in about the year 1500 B.C., when a subterranean volcano erupted. Scientists estimate the enormous energy released at the time of the catastrophe to be equivalent to the blast from a 400-megaton nuclear bomb. The vast hail storm of molten rock fragments from the gigantic blowup fell on surrounding lands within a radius of 100 miles, making them uninhabitable. This, some authorities believe, explains the sudden disappearance from history of the once-great Minoan civilization in the second millenium B.C. They are inclined to identify the lengendary Atlantean kingdom with the sea empire of Minoan Crete.

Most occultists and some archeologists disagree. They point out that while there are a few resemblances between Plato's description of Atlantis and the archaeological finds of Santorini, there are also irreconcilable differences. Data derived from psychic sources for the most part locate the lost continent in the Atlantic ocean.

The problem will be resolved, should some of the predictions made by seers regarding the future re-emergence of Atlantis come true.

The best known of these forecasts is that of Edgar Cayce, the "Sleeping Prophet" of Virginia Beach. In one of his trance readings, given on June 28, 1940, Cayce prophesied:

> "Poseidia will be one of the first parts of Atlantis to rise again. Expect it in '68 and '69. Not so far away!"

The fact that Cayce was wrong about his dates—Atlantis did not surface in 1968 or 1969—does not trouble those who believe in the essential accuracy of his predictions. They point out that it has always been difficult to pinpoint dates in prophecy, and are certain that Atlantis will rise again, just as Cayce has foretold.

The seer identified Poseidia as a submerged Atlantean island in the vicinity of the Bahamas. While no part of sunken Atlantis ever resurfaced in 1968, in that year an underwater archeological exploration did discover on the ocean floor off the coast of Bimini (too small Bahamian islands) mysterious pavements and sunken columns, which may once have formed part of an engulfed city—perhaps a public building or temple.

Atlantists who believe in the validity of prophecy

point out that in one of his trance readings, Cayce said that when Poseidia rises off the Bahamas, the remains of an Atlantean temple will be uncovered.

According to Cayce, the reappearance of Atlantis will initiate a series of catastrophic changes in the earth's structure and activity. These violent upheavals will occur first in the South Pacific and in the Mediterranean area, but later will spread to other regions of the globe.

In another reading, Cayce predicted that "portions of the now east coast of New York, or New York City itself, will in the main disappear. This will be in another generation . . . while the southern portions of Carolina, Georgia—these will disappear. This will be much sooner."

Cayce's description of Atlantean civilization includes achievements not mentioned in Plato's work—scientific wonders that Plato himself could never have envisioned. The prophet of Virginia Beach said that the Atlanteans lighted their homes with electricity, had elevators in their buildings, developed radio and television, and had amphibian aircraft.

Cayce said the Atlanteans developed a "Great Crystal" which was used as an oracle to receive communications from God. It was also used to convert solar energy into healing rays which could be employed to regenerate the human body and to prolong the lifespan. The Great Crystal could also be tuned to a powerful negative pitch which could be used destructively. It was misuse of that great power that brought about the catastrophe which resulted in the submergence of Atlantis.

Charles Berlitz, explorer-author of a book entitled *Without a Trace*, published in 1977, advances the theory that the lost capital of Atlantis may be in the center of that mysterious area known as the Bermuda Triangle. He reported the finding of a submerged pyramid

500 feet high and as many feet at the base, rising from the ocean's floor.

He told an interviewer that the huge structure was accidentally located by some equipment that he and some friends were using to search for banks where fish live.

> "The sonar marked a straight line, sloping upward and then down again," Berlitz said.
>
> "My friends thought it was a subterranean mountain. Well, we went out later and zeroed in on it. It had four sloping walls, perfectly aligned, very much like the pyramids of Egypt. I haven't been down there to see whether it's built of stone, but in my opinion, it is a pyramid."

BEAUREGARD, PERE.   A Parisian priest, who prophesied the coming of the French Revolution thirteen
years before it occurred. During a sermon delivered
from the pulpit of the Notre Dame Cathedral, it is said,
he told his congregation in 1789:

> "Yes, Lord, Thy temple will be plundered and
> devastated, Thy festivals abolished. Thy name
> blasphemed, Thy service proscribed. But what
> do I hear, great God, what do I see? Instead of
> hymns in Thy praise, O Lord, with which this
> sacred roof resounded, profane, licentious songs
> are sung. And you, infamous goddess of pagan-
> ism, abandoned Venus, you have the audacity to
> enter here, usurp the place of the living God,
> seat yourself on the throne of the Holiest of Holy,
> and receive the blasphemous idolatry of your true
> worshippers."

All of which came true.

BERDYAEV, NICHOLAS (1874–1948).   Best known as a philosopher-theologian of the existentialist school, Berdyaev was also a mystic. A native of Kiev, he was at first identified with the socialist movement in Russia, a struggle which he himself described as being waged "with the daring and mercilessness of green youth."

As he came from an aristocratic family, this meant rebelling against his own social class. He was arrested for taking part in a mass demonstration staged by the revolutionaries, and sentenced to exile for three years. Later he repudiated Communism and Marxism. In 1922, the Soviet government arrested him and sentenced him to deportation. He settled first in Berlin, but later moved to Paris, where he spent the remainder of his life.

Berdyaev wrote numerous books and articles, only part of which have been translated into English. A philosopher of being, one of his chief preoccupations was time, "which loses itself in eternity, and of time which precipitates itself toward an end which is not death, but transformation."

He believed that all human activity is part of a prophetic pattern. He wrote:

> "The philosophy of history cannot but be prophetic, revealing the secrets of the future."

In a prophetic work entitled *The End of Our Time*, first published in 1923, Berdyaev foresees the coming of chaotic changes in the world's societies, as Western civilization moves toward the day's end into the nighttime of its history, which he calls the new Middle Ages.

> "The new Middle Ages will be, inevitably and in the highest degree, 'of the people'—and not in the least democratic.
> "Power will be strong, often dictatorial . . . Life will

become more austere, without its modern showiness. A very strong tension will be set up for the human spirit, and a particular sort of monastic life in the world, a kind of new religious order, may emerge. . . Work must be understood as a participation in creation, and great occupational activity combined with a cutting-down of 'wants' will characterize the whole of society in this new period of history. It is only thus that impoverished mankind can continue to exist . . . The notion of 'progress' will be discarded as camouflaging the true ends of life, there will be creation, there will be turning to God or to Satan . . . We must decrease the speed of that ever-moving current which is bearing us on to nothingness, and acquire a taste for eternity. But parallel to all this another force will be at work whose object will be the spread of sham civilization, and that will be the spirit of Antichrist. . . .

". . . Women will be very much to the fore in the new Middle Ages . . . Woman is bound more closely than man to the soul of the world and its primary elemental forces, and it is through her that he reaches communion with them . . . Women are filling a notably important role in the present religious revival; as in the gospel, they are predestined to be the myrrh-bearers. Day is the time of the exclusive predominance of masculine culture; at night (the Middle Ages) the feminine element receives her rights.

"This extended activity of women in the future does not at all mean a development of that 'women's emancipation' with which we are familiar, the end and method of which is to reduce woman to the likeness of man by leading her along a masculine road . . . It is the *eternal feminine* that has

so great a future in coming history, not the eman-
cipated woman. . . .

". . . This means finding the mystical meaning of
love, of a transfiguring love that looks not to time
but to eternity. Here we cross the frontier of modern history and leave the rational day to enter
the dark night of the Middle Ages . . .

". . . We are remaking the atmosphere, so foreign
to modern history, and so make possible the return of magic, black and white. And there is, too,
the renewal of impassioned discussions of the
mysteries of the divine life. So we go from an age
that was animistic to one that will be spiritual.
But the future is doubtful . . . I have a presenti-
ment that an outbreak of the powers of evil is at
hand . . . The night is coming and we must take up
spiritual weapons for the fight against evil, we
must make more sensitive our power for its discernment, we must build up a new knighthood.

"The flood waxes and bears us on / to a dark
immensity . . . / there where we sail, all around
us / the flaming abyss."

BEROSUS.   A Chaldean priest, astrologer and historian
of the second century B.C. As a monument to his remarkable talents as a prophet, nearly all of whose predictions were fulfilled, the Greeks erected a statue of
him in Athens, which had a gilded tongue symbolizing
the truth and accuracy of his forecasts.

Berosus translated into Greek the basic Babylonian
works on astrology, a science at which the Chaldeans
excelled. So profound and comprehensive was their
study of the stars that the compiled records of celestial
configurations for periods are variously estimated at be-

tween 370,000 and 720,000 years. (The first figure is one given by Cicero, the latter by Berosus himself.)

In addition to his works on astrology, Berosus also compiled and translated into Greek a three-volume history of Babylonia in which he transcribed from local sources of the time the Chaldean account of the Flood.

Although none of his works have survived in their original form, extracts have been preserved in the books of later writers who derived them directly from the original.

Berosus, in common with almost all prophets of whatever period in human history, foresaw the eventual destruction of all things on earth in a final great cataclysm. He predicted that the fiery end would come according to the inevitable movement of the stars and planets.

"When all the planets conjoin in the sign of Cancer," he declared, "and are so positioned that a straight line would pass directly through all their orbs, all things terrestrial will be consumed."

BLAKE, WILLIAM (1757–1827). English artist, visionary and poet, born in London on November 28, 1757. The strong strain of mysticism that was to dominate his later life and work manifested itself early when, at the age of four, Blake "saw God put his forehead to the window." When he was only seven, he reported seeing a tree filled with angels.

Throughout his life, he possessed a "second sight" that made the invisible world a part of his daily experience. At all times, even during routine tasks, he felt himself surrounded by "celestial inhabitants," many of whom he incorporated in his drawings.

Blake's output, both graphic and literary, was prodigious. But, owing to the mystical character of both, the exact meaning of his words and pictures has remained obscure even to this day.

During his lifetime, Blake received little recognition, and following his death in 1827, his name was forgotten for three decades.

One of his most powerful prophetic works was the poem on America, *A Prophecy*:

> "Sound! sound! my loud war-trumpets, and alarm my Thirteen Angels! / Loud howls the eternal Wolf! the eternal Lion lashes his tail! / America is darken'd; and my punishing Demons, terrified, / Crouch howling before their caverns deep, like skins dried in the wind.
>
> "They cannot smite the wheat, nor quench the fatness of the earth: / They cannot smite with sorrows, nor subdue the plow and spade; / They cannot wall the city, nor moat round the castle of princes; / They cannot bring the stubbed oak to overgrow the hills; / For terrible men stand on the shores, & in their robes I see / Children take shelter from the lightnings: there stands Washington / And Paine and Warren with their foreheads reared toward the east."
>
> "Stiff shudderings shook the heav'nly thrones! France, Spain & Italy / In terror viewed the bands of Albion, and the ancient Guardians, / Fainting upon the elements, smitten with their own plagues. / They slow advance to shut the five gates of their law built heaven, / Filled with blasting fancies and with mildews of despair, / With fierce disease and lust, unable to stem the fires of Orc. / But the five gates were consumed, & their bolts and hinges melted; / And the fierce flames

burnt round the heavens, & round the abodes of men."

BLAVATSKY, HELENA PETROVNA (1831–1891). Noted modern occultist and founder of the Theosophical Society; was born at Ekaterinoslav, Russia.

When she was 17 years old, she married Nicephore Blavatsky, a councillor of state, from whom she soon separated. Afterwards, she traveled throughout the world, visiting Canada, the U.S., Mexico and India.

She settled in New York in 1873, where she became prominent in spiritualist circles. During this period, she met Col. H. S. Olcott, with whom she founded the Theosophical Society. Later, she and Col. Olcott established the Society's headquarters at Adyar, near the city of Madras, India, where it still functions at the present time.

Madame Blavatsky produced a large body of literature on occult subjects, her principal work being *The Secret Doctrine*, published in 1888.

She accurately predicted that between 1888 and 1897, "materialistic science will receive a death blow" because "one by one, facts and processes in Nature's workshops are permitted to find their way into the exact sciences, while mysterious help is given to rare individuals in unravelling its arcana."

During the period designated by Madame Blavatsky, Roentgen discovered the x-ray; Mme. Curie, radio-activity; and Hendrik Lorentz, the electron. All these advances in science required a re-examination of basic materialistic concepts in physics, which prevailed at the time.

In her prevision of future developments on this planet, Madame Blavatsky predicted the eventual disappearance of what in her day was called the Aryan race and the coming of what she termed the Sixth Root-Race. She spoke of a series of cataclysms "which must one day destroy Europe . . . as also most of the lands directly connected with the confines of our continent and isles."

> "When shall this be? Who knows save the Great Masters of Wisdom (the Mahatmas), perchance, and they are as silent upon the subject as the snow-capped peaks that tower above them. All that we know is that it will silently come into existence . . . The exultant pulse will beat high in the heart of the new race in the American zone, but there will be no Americans when the sixth race commences; no more, in fact, than Europeans; for they will become *a new race, and many new nations* . . .
>
> "Thus it is the mankind of the New World. . . . whose mission and Karma it is to sow the seeds for a forthcoming, grander, and far more glorious Race than any of those we know of at present. The cycles of Matter will be succeeded by cycles of spirituality and a fully developed mind. . . ."

BOSCO, ST. JOHN (1815–1888). Founder of the two religious orders, the Salesians, and the Salesian Sisters, Don Bosco (as he was familiarly known) was born near Turin, Italy on August 16, 1815. His father died when he was two years of age, and he was reared by his mother, a pious, hardworking woman, who was still employed as a housekeeper at the time of her death.

Following his ordination in 1841, Don Bosco began his lifelong career as counselor and educator of homeless youth. Various miracles were attributed to him. He was canonized by Pope Pius XI on April 1, 1934.

He was endowed with a prophetic gift, especially as it concerned the future of the Church and the Papacy. He cautioned his admirers, however,

> "Do not call me a prophet until the things I have foretold have come to pass."

In one of his premonitory visions, Don Bosco foresaw a time of desolation in Rome, when the Pope would be forced to flee the Vatican with a band of faithful. His account of the revelation in part follows:

> "There was a dark night, when men were no longer able to make out which road they should take to return to their past. Then there appeared in the sky a most magnificent light which revealed the road to the travellers as if it were midday. In that moment a multitude of people were seen, women, men, girls, monks, nuns and priests with the Pope at the head, coming out of the Vatican and taking up the form of a procession.
>
> "But behold, a furious storm broke out, which obscured the light somewhat, and a battle seemed to break out between the light and dark. Meanwhile the procession reached a small square covered with dead and wounded, who appeared to be crying for help in a loud voice.
>
> "The lines of the procession began to break up. After walking for a space of time which corresponds to two hundred sunrises, everyone realized that they were no longer in Rome. Alarm spread through the minds of everyone and everyone rallied round the Pope to guard his person and to help him in his needs.
>
> "At that minute two angels were seen carrying a standard who went towards the Pope saying 'Receive the standard of He who fought and dis-

persed the most powerful people on Earth. Your enemies will be defeated and your sons will shed tears and will call for your return with sighs.' Carrying the standard they could see that on one side was written *Regina sine labe concepta* (the Queen immaculately conceived) and on the other *Auxilium cristianorum* (the Help of Christians). "The Pope took the standard with joy, but gazed attentively at the small number of those who remained around him and became saddened by it."

Two angels arrived on the scene and instructed the Pontiff to return to the Vatican and to "write to your brothers throughout the world, telling them that it is necessary to bring about a reform of both customs and people themselves. If that is not achieved, the bread of the Divine word will not be broken among the people."

When the Pope heard this, he turned back toward Rome, and the length of the procession following him began to grow.

"When they set foot in the Holy City they wept for the desolation and for the citizens as so many of them were dead. They re-entered St. Peter's intoning the Te Deum which was taken up by a choir of angels singing, 'Glory to God in the Highest and in Earth Peace among men of good will.' When the singing had come to an end, the darkness disappeared completely and a brilliant sun shone out.

"The city, the countryside and the landscape were much denuded of population, the ground was churned up as if by a hurricane, a heavy shower and hail, and the people were arguing with spirit one against the other saying, "God in Israel.""

"From the beginning of the exile until the singing of the Te Deum the sun will rise two hundred times. The whole time that will elapse while these things are completed will correspond to four hundred sunrises."

BOUQUILLON, BERTINE.   A 19th century nun who devoted her life to nursing the sick at the Hôpital de St. Louis in St. Omer, France. Because of her piety and reputation for saintliness, her prophecies were highly respected during her lifetime, but have not been widely circulated outside Europe.

She predicted that the coming of the Antichrist and the pre-apocalyptic era would not occur in her own century but "will surely come in the next."

In a prophecy of 1850, she declared that even the nuns of her order would succumb to the powerful influence of the Antichrist:

"The end of time is not far off, and the Antichrist will not delay his coming. We shall not see him and not even the nuns who will follow him, but those who will come later will fall under his domination. When he comes, nothing will be changed, in the nunnery everyone will be dressed as usual; the religious exercises and the services will go on as usual . . . when the sisters will realize that Antichrist is in charge."

BRAHAN SEER. (Coinneach Odhar, or Kenneth Ore). A half-lengendary prophet of the Highlands of Scotland, who is believed to have flourished during the first part of the seventeenth century. Most of the prophecies and wise sayings attributed to him are related to the history of Scotland, its kings and some of the country's noble families, notably the Seaforths, whose principal seat was near Dingwall. The seer's birthplace is said to be Baile-na-Cille on the island of Lews. Nothing is known of his early life, save that he worked as a common laborer on a farm. According to tradition, he showed an unusual degree of intelligence and wit for one in his menial station.

Alexander Mackenzie, who in 1888 wrote a work on the seer's life and prophecies, says that when Coinneach was just entering his teens, he acquired a magical stone by which he could reveal the future destiny of man.

There are several versions of the manner in which the prophetic stone came into his possession. Mackenzie gives the following:

> "His mistress, the farmer's wife, was unusually exacting with him, and he, in return, continually teased her, and, on many occasions, expended much of his natural wit upon her, much to her annoyance and chagrin. Latterly, his conduct became so unbearable that she decided upon disposing of him in a manner which would save her any future annoyance. On one occasion, his master having sent him away to cut peats, which in those days were, as they now are in more remote districts, the common article of fuel, it was necessary to send him his dinner, he being too far from the house to come home to his meals, and the farmer's wife so far carried out her intention of destroying him, that she poisoned his dinner. It was somewhat late in arriving, and the future prophet, feeling exhausted from his honest exertions in his master's interest and from want of food, lay down on the hearth and fell into a heavy slumber. In this position he was suddenly awakened by feel-

ing something cold in his breast, which on exam-
ination he found to be a small white stone, with a
hole through the centre. He looked through it,
when a vision appeared to him which revealed the
treachery and diabolical intention of his mistress.
To test the truth of the vision, he gave the dinner
intended for himself to his faithful collie; the poor
brute writhed, and died soon after in the greatest
agony.

Another legend adds that though the stone conferred
upon him a supernatural power of precognition, it had,
the first time he used it, deprived him of the sight of
that eye with which he had looked through it, and that
even afterward he was *cam* or blind in one eye.

BRIDGIT OF SWEDEN. (1302–1373).   The daughter of
Birger Persson, prince of the blood-royal of Sweden,
Bridgit (or Brigitta) was mute during the first three
years of her life, and her parents feared that she would
never be able to speak. However, she suddenly began to
talk with the facility and clarity of a person much
older than her years.
   Bridgit's mother, a singularly devout woman, died
soon after Bridgit started to speak, and her father sent
her to live with an aunt.
   At the age of 16, she married Ulpho Gudmarson, a
nobleman of Nericia, Sweden, to whom she bore eight
children.
   After the death of her husband following a joint
pilgrimage to the shrine of the Apostle James in San-
tiago de Compostela in Spain, Bridgit divided the family
property among her children and founded a convent in
Wastein, where she retired to devote herself entirely to
a religious life.
   She began to experience visions similar to some she

had known in early childhood, except that now they were more vivid and more frequent. These were written down and published, and enjoyed a wide popularity during the middle ages.

In 1350, she went to Rome, where she lived as a cloistered religious, wearing a coarse hair-shirt and fasting every Friday.

She remained in Rome until her death, with the exception of several pilgrimages, including one to Jerusalem where, in one of her visions, she foresaw the coming devastation by war of Cyprus.

Bridgit was canonized by Pope Boniface IX in 1391 and is still regarded as one of the patron saints of Sweden.

Her revelations, which are largely concerned with demonology, casuistry, and medieval theology, exercised a powerful influence over her contemporaries, but hold little of interest for the modern student.

CAESARIUS, ST. OF ARLES (A.D. 470–542).   Erudite ecclesiastic and bishop of Arles, was born at Chalons, Burgundy in A.D. 470. He was a leading figure in helping to shape the laws of the Church, and convoked various Councils at which important problems of canon law, theology, and education of the clergy were deliberated.

The prophetic work attributed to him was not discovered until 1789, when it was found among the documents of the last archbishop of Arles, Monsignor Du Lau.

The prophecy, written in Latin, covers a time span of centuries, starting with Caesarius's own century and extending to the time of the Great Monarch of the last days. Among the predictions included in the works are those foreshadowing the Crusades, the Black Death epidemic which devastated Europe in the 14th century, and the rise of Napoleon.

He foresees the eventual destruction of Paris by fire,

during the reign of a future antichrist. "The Gallic Babylon," he writes, "will be besieged by iron and fire, and will be brought down by a great conflagration, and inundated with flood. Afterward, other large cities of France will be destroyed."

Unlike most apocalyptic visions, however, that of Caesarius ends on an optimistic note:

"Then will shine forth the effulgence of divine mercy, supreme justice having punished all evildoers."

CALVAT, MELANIE (1831–1940).   Known as the little shepherdess of La Salette, Melanie Calvat was born at Isere, France, on November 7, 1831. She was the daughter of a stonemason named Pierre Calvat.

The prophetic messages she later revealed to the world came to her in visions in which the Holy Virgin appeared and spoke to her on September 19, 1846, when she was fourteen years of age.

According to published accounts of the event, Melanie and a companion named Maximine Giraud were descending a slope toward a small spring in the mountains of the commune of La Salette, near Grenoble, France, when they saw below them a luminous ball. "It looked as though the sun had fallen there," Melanie said afterward.

The luminous globe parted and from it appeared "a beautiful lady, all light and flowers." She sat down upon one of the stones ringing the spring and bent forward, her head held in her hands, in an attitude of great sorrow.

Presently, as the two children watched, the lady arose and was lifted into the air, where she remained suspended, her white habit resplendent with pearls.

She then spoke, entrusting the children with a

lengthy prophecy, and a warning to mankind. Her message concerned the decline of spiritual life and the corruption of the clergy; it foretold terrible, sometimes fratricidal, wars; the coming of the Antichrist, the destruction of many cities, including Paris and Rome; and major upheavals in nature.

"At the first blow of the sword of God, which will fall like lightning on humanity, the mountains and all nature will tremble because of the disorder and the misdeeds of men, which will rise to the very heavens.

"Paris will be destroyed by fire and Marseilles will be inundated by the sea. Other great cities will also be destroyed by fire—razed to the ground by fire. The just will have to suffer much; their prayers, penitence and tears will rise to heaven; all the people of God will pray for pardon and sing songs asking for compassion, and they will come to me for my intercession and my help.

"A period of peace will follow, but only for the space of twenty-five years. Then a forerunner of the Antichrist will marshal an army of men drawn from many nations, united under his banner. He will lead them in a bloody war against those still faithful to the living God.

"The earth will tremble and you yourselves will also quake if you are dedicated to the service of Jesus Christ on the surface, but inside have only self-admiration. Tremble! The Lord is on the point of delivering you into the hands of your enemies. . ."

"The seasons will change their intrinsic character; earth will be lit by a fiendish red light; water and fire will cause terrible seismic movements which will engulf mountains and cities.

"Rome will lose the faith and become the seat of Antichrist. The demons ailled to Antichrist will operate on the earth and in the sky, and humanity will become even more evil. But God will not forsake his truly faithful servants who are men of good will. The Gospel will be preached everywhere to all people and the nations will know the truth."

"Fight, Sons of Light, you small number who see; because the time of times, the final end, is near.

"The Church will remain in the dark; the world will be convulsed, but in this confusion, Enoch and Elijah will appear, full of the spirit of God. They will preach, and in their words will be the power of God; and men of good will will believe in God. Many spirits will be consoled; in virtue of the Holy Spirit, they will make great progress, and will condemn the diabolical deceptions of the Antichrist.

"Woe to the inhabitants of the earth! There will be sanguinary war, hunger, pestilence and epidemics, terrible rains of insects, thunder that will shake entire cities, earthquakes which will make entire regions uninhabitable. Voices will be heard in the air, and men will strike their heads against the wall, wishing for death, but this will only bring them, for their part, terrible torture. Blood will flow everywhere. Who could ever know victory unless God shortened the time of trial?

"Enoch and Elijah will be put to death. Pagan Rome will be destroyed, and fire will fall from heaven, destroying three cities. The sun will be darkened, and only the faith will survive.

"The time is at hand. The abyss is opening; the king of the kings of darkness is watching; the beast is watching with his subjects, who will proclaim him 'savior of the world.' He will rise superbly into the air, hoping to reach the sky; but the breath of the archangel Michael will kill him. He will fall back and the earth will shake without ceasing for three days. It will then open its womb full of fire and the beast and his followers will be admitted into the eternal abyss of the inferno. Then water and fire will purify the earth, and destroy all human pride. Everything will be renewed."

CANORI, ELISABETTA (1774–1825).   The Venerable Elisabetta Canori was born near Rome, Italy, on November 21, 1724. Very early in life, she showed mystical tendencies. Later, she entered a Trinitarian order.

All during her lifetime, Elisabetta enjoyed a reputation for sanctity and as "a living saint" was often asked for her prayers by the people of Rome, as well as by her immediate associates.

Her recorded prophecies are similar to others made before and after her time by religious visionaries: the decline and future regeneration of the Holy Faith; and the terrible punishments that await the wicked.

In a vision of December 10, 1815, she saw the Catholic Church symbolized as a venerable old lady, richly attired and adorned with jewels. But her face was full of sadness, and she cried out to God to intervene on behalf of her sons to save them from the terrors that would overwhelm them in the future.

The matriarchal figure of Elisabetta's vision was reduced to a humble state, stripped of her jewels and resplendent robes by three angels. As she swayed and almost fell from weakness, God set the cap of a noble matron upon her head and enveloped her in his splendor. "She sent out powerful rays of light to the four cardinal points of the compass. . . The inhabitants of the earth, dazzled by the brilliance of the light, and as if awakened from a profound dream, arose and leaving the darkness of their error, ran towards the light of the gospel."

CATACLYSMS AND NATURAL DISASTERS.   A common theme, running through nearly all prophecies, ancient or modern, is a warning of future cataclysms.

Earthquakes, fires, floods, climatic changes, reversal of the earth's magnetic poles, volcanic eruptions, collision with bodies from outer space—these and other calamities involving natural phenomena on a prodigious scale leave little room for optimism about the future.

This consistency may be due in part to an inherited memory of catastrophes that have occurred in the past, memories lodged in what Carl Jung called the collective unconscious.

On the other hand, it could represent a true precognition of similar disasters which we may reasonably expect to happen again in the future; or a combination of both.

Isaiah was one of the first major prophets to predict a violent paroxysm of nature, awaiting man on the far horizon of history. His words have a powerful, gripping simplicity:

"The earth shall reel to and fro like a drunkard. . ."

If taken literally, the catastrophe he describes would be of a magnitude unknown to recorded history. However, most scientists agree that a study of the earth's great mountain chains has produced evidence which suggests the occurrence in the remote past of upheavals of such indescribable violence that, as the German geophysicist Eduard Suess put it, "the imagination refuses to follow the understanding."

One result of these telluric convulsions, in which thousands of square miles of earth suddenly heaved upward, must have been gigantic earthquakes that would certainly have made the earth stagger like a drunken man. Even the most severe seismic shocks experienced today are but slight tremors compared to them.

In his celebrated prophecies, Nostradamus predicts various earth changes that will affect all parts of the globe. He speaks darkly of great floods and universal conflagrations, without giving any specific dates on which they will occur.

> "There shall occur in the month of October a great upheaval, such that all will believe the earth has lost it natural motion and plunged into everlasting darkness."

In another place, Nostradamus implies that the waters of the sea will rise suddenly to submerge the lower part of Italy, including the city of Rome.

His successors down to the present day have continued to prophesy in a similar vein. The best-known and most dramatic by far of the latter-day predictions are those of Edgar Cayce. A few typical examples follow:

In one of his trance readings, Cayce moved forward in time to the year 2100. He found himself traveling in a large, cigar-shaped aircraft, which attained velocities unheard of today. Upon landing at an airfield near the ruins of what had once been a huge metropolis, Cayce asked where he was. Regarding him with some surprise, a crew member told him they were in New York. Work was going forward in reconstruction of the devastated city.

Sometime in the 40-year period between 1958 and 1998, he said during another reading, the most overwhelming natural disaster in the history of North America will occur along the Atlantic coast in the area of New York and Connecticut. Even before that time—probably between 1978 and 1980—devastating earthquakes will destroy the cities of Los Angeles and San Francisco; and much of the Southern California coastline will be submerged.

Other Cayce readings foretell a shifting of the earth's axis by the year 2001, resulting in major climatic changes. Areas that have been frigid or semitropical "will become more tropical, and moss and fern will grow."

Immanuel Velikovsky maintains, probably correctly, that such a displacement of the earth's poles would require tremendous forces that could not come from the earth itself, but would have to be exerted from outer space. The explanation offered by scientists in the past for such a shift—that is, geological processes, such as redistribution of weight on the earth's surface, caused by a sudden elevation of mountainous masses —would appear to be inadequate.

Velikovsky's working hypothesis of what happened in the past, and might conceivably happen in the future, is terrifying. He says:

"Let us assume. . . that under the impact of a force or influence of an agent—and the earth does not travel in an empty universe—the axis of the earth shifted or tilted. At that moment an earthquake would make the globe shudder. Air and water would continue to move through inertia; hurricanes would sweep the earth and the seas would rush over continents, carrying gravel and sand and marine animals, and casting them on the land. Heat would be developed, rocks would melt, volcanoes would erupt, lava would flow from fissures in the ruptured ground, and cover vast areas. Mountains would spring up from the plains and would travel and climb on the shoulders of other mountains, causing faults and rifts. Lakes would be tilted and emptied; rivers would change their beds; large land areas with all their inhabitants would slip under the sea. Forests would burn, and the hurricanes and wild seas would wrest them from the ground on which they grew and pile them, branch and root, in large heaps. Seas would turn into deserts, their waters rolling away.

"And if a change in the velocity of the diurnal rotation—slowing it down—should accompany the shifting of the axis, the water confined to the equatorial oceans by centrifugal force would retreat to the poles, and high tides and hurricanes would rush from pole to pole, carrying reindeer and seals to the tropics, and desert lions into the Arctic, moving from the equator up to the mountain ridges of the Himalayas and down the African jungles; and crumbled rocks torn from splintering mountains would be scattered over large distances; and herds of animals would be washed from the plains of Siberia."*

Among other catastrophes predicted by Cayce are: the sinking of a part of Japan; major geological disturbances in the South Pacific and in the Mediterranean; and the rising of the sea's floor off the Bahamian coasts.

* Immanuel Velikovsky, *Earth in Upheaval.* New York, 1955.

A geologist who made a study of Cayce's predictions regarding earth changes commented that while some of them were scientiflcally feasible, such changes occur gradually rather than precipitously as described by the prophet.

Some of the *possible* changes extrapolated by scientific futurists tend to support the doomsday visionaries, at least in part. In 1974, for example, two prominent astronomers—John Gribbin and Stephen Plagemann— warned that the earth might experience a series of devastating events, starting in 1982.

In that year, they said, all nine planets of the solar system will be aligned on the same side of the sun along a straight axis. Such a planetary line-up, called the Jupiter Effect, could easily trigger major earthquakes, not only in California, but in other areas of the world as well.

Their rationale for such a prediction was this:

The 1982 planetary alignment would come at a time when the sun was at a peak of a sunspot cycle, causing a great surge in the sun's magnetic activity. The result would be violent solar storms. These bursts of solar activity could change the wind directions and modify temperature patterns, thus slowing down the speed of the earth's rotation. The consequence of such a reduction would be a jolt to the whole globe, setting off earthquakes in those areas of the world already under geological stress.

The astronomer team wrote in their book, *The Jupiter Effect*:

> "One region where one of the greatest fault systems lies today under a great strain, long overdue for a giant leap forward and just waiting for the necessary kick, is California."

Even without the added nudge of the Jupiter Effect, the influence of solar flares alone can trigger earthquakes, according to J. F. Simpson of the Goodyear Aerospace Corporation, who analyzed records of 22,561 earthquakes over the past thirteen and one-half years.

He found that maximum earthquake frequency occurred at times of high solar activity, especially when this activity was rapidly episodal. He suggested that solar flares may cause abrupt changes in the speed of the earth's rotation, which in turn might induce temporary stresses, placing a critical strain on parts of the earth's crust already weakened by existing deformation.

CAYCE, EDGAR (1877–1945).   The best-known prophet and psychic of the twentieth century was born March 18, 1877, in Hopkinsville, Kentucky.

As a young man, Cayce worked first as a bookseller and later as a photographer. The first intimation he had of his psychic gift occurred when he was healed overnight of a throat ailment which he had endured for nearly ten months. The cure was effected while he was in a self-induced trance state.

Cayce first became famous for his strange ability to diagnose human ills, even in patients who were far distant. Although he had only an elementary education, during his trance states he spoke with authority in medical terms. He not only diagnosed difficult cases which had baffled professional practitioners, but prescribed effective treatment for the diseases.

Upon waking from his trance, Cayce would not recall anything he had said during the sleep interval. A simple man, who knew nothing of the occult, and who was a church-going, fundamentalist Christian, he did not pretend to understand his strange powers.

Cayce's son, Hugh Lynn, has described the procedure followed by his father each time he gave a reading. "At the appointed time, Edgar Cayce would come in from his garden or from fishing, or from working in his office. He would loosen his tie, shoelaces, cuffs, and belt, and lie down on a couch. His hands, palms up over his forehead, were later crossed palms down over his abdomen. He would breathe deeply a few times. When his eyelids began to flutter, it was necessary to read to him a suggestion-formula which had been secured in a reading in answer to the request, "Give the proper suggestion to be given Edgar Cayce to secure a physical reading." It was necessary to watch the eyelids carefully. If they were allowed to flicker too long before the suggestion was read, my father would not respond. He might then sleep for a couple of hours or more and awaken refreshed without knowing he hadn't given a reading."

Although Cayce's most amazing feats were those involving medical diagnosis and treatment, he began to answer other kinds of questions regarding people's past lives, future earth changes and coming cataclysms, and so on.

Many of these prophecies were linked in one way or another with the sunken continent of Atlantis which is referred to 700 times in Cayce's recorded readings.

The messages describe in detail the great achievements of the Atlantean civilization before the last island remnants of the lost continent sank beneath the sea some 10,000 years ago. (See article under *Atlantis*.)

Cayce reported that materialists of the Atlantean culture, who gained a dominant position in their society, destroyed their world by accident, through tuning a Great Crystal which focused solar energy, to a point beyond what atomic scientists today would call criticality, inducing volcanic activity that brought on the final catastrophe which destroyed Atlantis.

In all, Cayce gave 14,256 readings, which are pre-served in the archives of the Edgar Cayce Foundation and the Association for Research and Enlightenment, Inc., at Virginia Beach, Va. After the prophet's death in 1945, his son became first director and then chair-man of the Boards of both nonprofit organizations, which continue to conduct experiments and research based on data produced by the Edgar Cayce readings.

CAZOTTE, JACQUES (1720–1792).   A French poet and writer of romantic novels, to whom is attributed the famous *Prophétie de Cazotte*, which foretold the French Revolution and the fate of some of his friends who would take part in it.

He was born at Dijon and educated by the Jesuits. While still a young man, he joined the brotherhood known as the Illuminati, the members of which prac-ticed occult arts and claimed to possess wisdom com-municated to them directly from a higher source.

Soon afterward, Cazotte announced that he had at his command the power of prophecy.

Some scholars believe that Cazotte's dramatic ac-count of the horrors to be unleashed in the approaching Revolution was largely the invention of another writer —Jean Francois de La Harpe.

The *Prophétie* describes a dinner party which was given years before the Revolution, at which many no-tables and distinguished men of letters were present.

"The dinner was a gay one. The guests talked of everything—politics, religion, philosophy, and even the Deity. In those days, the philosophy of Voltaire carried everything before it. The party hailed with delight the progress of liberal ideas, and began to calculate the time when the great social revolution might be expected to take place.

There were some, like Bailly, who expressed a fear that, from their advanced age, they could not hope to witness it. One only of the guests remained sad and silent amid the general festivity. "It was Cazotte. 'Yes, gentlemen,' he broke silence at last, 'we shall all witness it, the great and sublime Revolution you anticipate: the decrees of Providence are immutable. The spirit teaches me that you will all witness it.' And he fell back into gloomy reverie.

" 'To to be sure, we all hope to witness, to take part in that great deliverance,' cried all the guests; 'a man need not be a prophet to tell us that.'

" 'A prophet! yes, I am one,' replied Cazotte, aroused by the word. 'I have witnessed within my mind the great tragedy of the Revolution; I know everything that will happen. Do you wish, gentlemen, to be told what your share in it is to be, whether as actors or spectators?'

" 'Come,' said Condorcet, with his usual sneering smile, 'attention! Habakkuk is going to speak.'

" 'As for you, M. de Condorcet,' continued Cazotte, 'you will die on the floor of a dungeon, maddened with the thought of having surrendered your country to the tyranny of brutal ignorance; you will die by poison, which you will take to avoid falling into the hands of the executioner.'

"The whole company was struck dumb. Cazotte turned to Chamfort. 'As for you, M. de Chamfort, you will open your veins in two-and-twenty places with a razor, and yet you will survive your two-and-twenty wounds two months.'

"Here Vicq d'Azyr began to chant the *De Profundis.*

" 'That is right, Vicq d'Azyr, it is time for you to

sing your own funeral hymn. You will not open your veins, for you will be afraid of your hand trembling. You will ask a friend to do you that kindness in order to make sure, and you will die in the middle of the night, in a fit of gout, and bathed in your blood. Stop, look at that clock, it is going to strike the hour of death.'

"The clock stood at a quarter to one. All the guests rose in their places in an involuntary movement. As they got up, Cazotte counted the victims like a shepherd telling off his flock. 'You will die on the scaffold,' he said to M. de Nicolai; 'and you, too, M. Bailly, and you, M. de Malesherbes, and you, M. Boucher. The scaffold or suicide—such is your fate! and six years will not pass over your heads before everything I have said shall come to pass.'

" 'Upon my word, you are dealing in miracles to-night,' said La Harpe, 'and you don't mean to let me have any share in them.'

" 'You will be the subject of a miracle fully as extraordinary. I see you beating your breast and kneeling humbly before the altar; I see you kissing the hand of one of those priests whom you now scoff at; I see you seeking for peace of mind in the shade of a cloister, and asking pardon for your sins at the confessional.'

" 'Ah! I am easy now,' cried Chamfort, 'if we none of us are to perish till La Harpe turns Christian!'

" 'We ladies shall be lucky, then,' observed the Duchess of Grammont, 'in having no share in this revolution. Of course, we shall take an interest in it; but it is understood that we are to be spared, and our sex will protect us, of course.'

" 'It may be so, but one thing is certain, that your Grace will be led to the scaffold, you and many other ladies with you in a cart, and with their hands tied.'

Cazotte continued: 'The last person executed will be —' Here he paused.

" 'Well! who is the happy mortal who is to enjoy that distinguished privilege?'

" 'It is the only one that will be left to the King of France.'

"After this prediction, since become so famous, adds his biographer, inasmuch as fate seemed to take a pleasure in fulfilling every word of it, Cazotte took his leave, and quitted the room, leaving the guests silent and awestruck.

"A certain M. de N. has inserted the following statement in the Parisian journals with reference to the above extraordinary prediction of M. Cazotte. He says 'that he was very well acquainted with this respectable old man, and had often heard him speak of the great distress which would befall France at a time when the people in every part of France lived in perfect security, and expected nothing of the kind.' M. de N. adds a remarkable fact, which is of itself sufficient to establish Cazotte's reputation for prevision. Everyone knows that his great attachment to the monarchy was the reason of his being sent to prison on the 2nd of September, 1792, and that he escaped from the murderers by the heroic courage of his daughter, who appeased the mob by the moving spectacle of her filial affection. The very same mob that would have put him to death, carried him home in triumph.

"All his friends came to congratulate him on his escape. M. D., who visited him, said to him: 'Now you are safe!' 'I believe not,' answered Cazotte, 'for in three days I shall be guillotined.'

"M. D. replied, 'How can that be?' Cazotte continued, 'Yes, my friend, in three days I shall die upon the scaffold. Here are papers which I am very anxious should be handed over to my wife; I request you to give them to her, and to console her.' M. D. declared that this was all folly, and left him with the conviction that his reason had suffered at the sight of the horrors he had escaped.

"The next day he went to see him again, but learned that a gendarme had conducted M. Cazotte to the municipality. Soon afterward he learned that his friend had been condemned and executed."

CHEIRO (COUNT LOUIS HAMON).   British clairvoyant, astrologer and palmist, who gained world renown as a prophet, owing to the accuracy of his predictions.

He pinpointed in surprising detail coming events in the lives of many celebrities. For example, in a series of predictions which he wrote in 1925, he said of Edward VIII, then Prince of Wales:

"It is within the range of possibility, owing to the peculiar planetary influences to which he is subjected, that he will fall victim of a devastating love affair. If he does, I predict that the Prince will give up everything, even the chance of being crowned, rather than lose the object of his affection."

As is well known, more than ten years after this forecast was published, the Prince of Wales ascended the throne of England upon the death of his father, George V, but was quickly embroiled in a constitutional fight with then Prime Minister Stanley Baldwin, who refused to sanction a morganatic marriage with twice-divorced Wallis Warfield Simpson. On December 11, 1936, Edward VIII abdicated in favor of his brother Albert, Duke of York, rather than give up "the object of his affection." As Duke of Windsor, he married Mrs. Simpson on June 3, 1937 and spent the remainder of his life with her in voluntary exile.

Cheiro forewarned William T. Stead, eminent English journalist, against making an ocean voyage in mid-April 1912. In a letter to Stead, he wrote: "Very critical and dangerous for you should be April 1912, especially about the middle of the month. So don't travel by water then if you can help it. If you do, you will be liable to meet with such danger to your life that the very worst may happen. I know I am not wrong about this water danger; I only hope I am, or at least that you won't be travelling somewhere about that period."

Stead ignored Cheiro's warning and on April 14, 1912 was among the passengers who went down with the *Titanic* when she struck an iceberg and sank during her maiden voyage.

Like Edgar Cayce and others, Cheiro foresaw the re-emergence of lost Atlantis. In the early 1920s, he predicted: "During the next fifty to a hundred years, after a series of devastating earthquakes, the islands of the Azores will rise from the Atlantic, and ruins of the long-lost continent of Atlantis will be discovered and explored."

Cheiro's prophecies were based in part upon his knowledge of astrology. He believed that the world was about to leave the age of Pisces and to enter the Aquarian age:

"By a knowledge of the precession of the equi-
noxes," he said, "science teaches us that it takes
2,150 years for the sun to retrograde through a
single sign of the Zodiac. At the time when Abraham, the father of the Hebrews, received 'the
promise' the sun was in the sign of Aries the
Ram; and in its beautiful, allegorical language,
the Bible gives us the picture of Abraham saving
his only son from the altar of sacrifice and offer-
ing up a ram in his stead.

"Two thousand, one hundred and fifty years later,
the Sun entered the sign of Pisces the Fishes, and
another great epoch opened in the history of the
world, when Christ selected fishermen to be his
disciples—to one of whom he promised he would
make him 'a fisher of men.' From that period,
which gave the dawn of Christianity, the fall of
Jerusalem and the dispersal of the Jews, a definite
milestone in history, 2,150 years has run its
course and we have already commenced the
period of the entry of the Sun into the Sign of
Aquarius, when the mysterious Aquarian age will
dawn across the world; and already its first rays
have revolutionized Russia, China, India, and
countries that come under its influence."

The seer spoke of the final war of Armageddon,
which would be brought about "by the return of
Judah and Israel to their country." He adds that in the
end it is only war that will save humanity. "It is only
when the world will be satiated with blood, destruction
and violence that it will wake from its present night-
mare of madness—and thus it is that the coming 'War
of Wars' fits into the design of things. Through intense
tribulation shall man be brought nearer to perfection
and more fitted to enjoy the wonders of the new Aquar-

ian age, that born in blood and sacrifice to Moloch, will in the end fulfill the meaning of its symbol, 'the Water Bearer' whose pouring out of water on the earth is the emblem of unselfishness—the negation of self— arrived at through suffering."

Cheiro correctly predicted the spread of Communism throughout the world during the latter half of the twentieth century:

> "During the coming years, the influence of Communism will spread through all countries; the most fantastic doctrines will be openly preached and absorbed by all classes. Rich men will give away their wealth and gladly become poor; kings will break bread with workers, and workers will dictate to kings; sons and daughters of the highest will become socialists, and the lands they inherit they will give to the people."

CHINA IN PROPHECY.   China, "the sleeping giant who has awakened," figures prominently both in inspired prophecies and in scientific futurism. Both foresee the probability of that country being involved in future atomic wars of annihilation.

Messianic prophecies, derived in a large measure from the Apocalypse of John, identify China as head of a future Asiastic confederacy (called "kings from the east") that will deploy a vast army of 200 million men to move against the Western forces commanded by a coming leader called the Roman Emperor.

Armies of that magnitude tax the imagination. At the same time, the rapid yearly increase in the populations of Asian countries makes such a figure less fantastic, if applied to the year 2000. It has been estimated that China alone will have a population of one billion by that date.

According to the revelations of John, the vast Oriental hordes will kill a third of mankind before eventually being defeated.

The contemporary French astrologer and prophet, Hades, sees China as a "dark and threatening cloud" over the future of the West. He identifies Pluto as China's planetary ruler, and observes that Pluto symbolizes a new civilization, based upon atomic power. "You can set the date," he writes, "Pluto in the sign of Scorpio in 1984–1999. Only after 1984 will China be in full possession of her power."

> "It will require a number of years for her to forge an industrial empire. [The country] has been engaged in this program since 1949, and activities especially in the field of atomic eneregy, have provided each of China's provinces with a center of nuclear studies, at the same time decentralizing the atomic industry. Our brilliant experts . . . have been amazed. I predict that in 1984, other 'brilliant experts' will be equally amazed."

Western scientific futurists and knowledgeable military planners appear to hold similar views. In a study made by Herman Kahn at the Rand Corporation's Center for International Studies, the analyst concludes:

> "It is clear that as soon as the Chinese develop adequate logistics and lines of communication, they will be a most formidable threat to all contiguous areas."

In any China-U.S. confrontation, Kahn points out, China would be in a better position than the U.S. to risk a limited nuclear war in which two or three major cities would be destroyed to get her way.

"Even if it were feasible to retaliate in kind without setting off the Doomsday Machine [total nuclear war that would destroy all life on the planet] the social and political impact of accepting such losses would raise much more serious internal and external problems in the United States than in China. It seems most likely, for example, that having to accept and explain the rationale of an exchange of two or three major U.S. cities for an equal number of Chinese cities would result in political suicide for the party in power in the U.S., plus some alliance instabilities, but only in some serious inconvenience to the Chinese government."

In a word, a future China, fully armed with total nuclear capability, will not be restrained by the humanitarian instincts which inhibit the people, if not the leaders, of most Western countries.

CORRAL, JOSE.   Spanish writer and student of prophecy who, in 1972, published a volume entitled *El fin del mundo está muy cerca* (The End of the World Is Very Near). His work is based chiefly upon the famous prophecy of St. Malachy, and upon a number of less-known prefigurations linking the Church and the papacy to future events in the history of the world.

At the conclusion of his perceptive analysis, Corral offers his own predictions for the years between 1970 and 2000, derived from his study of the sources covered in his book:

BETWEEN THE YEARS 1970 AND 1980:

1. Vacancy of the chair of Peter for a year and a half.

2. The Catholic clergy and members of religious or-

ders will, for the most part, abandon the wearing of ecclesiastical garb.

3. The election of two anti-popes, corresponding to those St. Malachy designated by the symbolic mottoes *De Medietate Lunae* and *De Labore Solis*. These two pontiffs will be the immediate sucessors of Pope Paul VI.

4. Prodigious signs in the heavens, involving the sun, moon and stars, which will herald the calamities described in the following paragraph.

5. The unleashing of a "partial" atomic war. Or it may be a gigantic earthquake that will affect an immense area of the globe. Of the two readings, Corral says he is inclined to the first. Several nations will be wiped out.

6. Election of a true pope, indicated in St. Malachy's prophecy by symbolic device, *De Gloria Olivae*. He will be erudite and saintly, and will bring about a reform of the Church.

7. The coronation, by this pope, of a king of the French royal family, who will rule most of the world and, together with the pontiff, will reform the globe.

8. The conversion of Russia and other nations to Christianity, as foreshadowed by the prophecy of Fatima and St. Paul in his Epistle to the Romans, 11:25.

9. Universal peace such as the world has never known.

BETWEEN THE YEARS 1995 AND 2000:

10. Advent of the Antichrist, who will make war against the faithful and conquer them.

11. World-wide apostasy.

12. Betrayal of the Church by the greater part of the clergy.

13. Celebration of the Eucharist will be suppressed for a period of three and one half years.

14. The unleashing of a total nuclear war which in a short time will destroy all animal and vegetable life on earth.

15. The prophets Elijah and Enoch will manifest themselves.

16. The seven last plagues, described in the *Apocalypse* of John will materialize.

17. Conversion of the Jews to Christianity.

18. Death of the Pope designated by the motto, *De Gloria Olivae*, and election of the final pope, Peter II of Rome.

19. Purification of the Great Sanctuary.

20. The destruction of Rome, marking the end of the world and the Last Judgment.

CUSA, CARDINAL NICHOLAS OF (1401–1464). Philosopher, visionary and theologian, was born at Cusa in the diocese of Treves, Germany, in 1401. He died in Todi, Italy on August 11, 1464.

At an early age, Nicholas joined the Brothers of the Common Life. He later read mathematics, law and philosophy at the University of Padua.

Although a capable organizer and church administrator, Nicholas was also a profound thinker and lucid writer. His writings generally follow the Neoplatonic Christian tradition, conceiving God as an absolute unity. To hold such a view distinguished him from his contemporaries, who adhered to the Catholic doctrine of the Trinity.

He prophesied that, owing to the corruption of the clergy, the Church would suffer a future decline, to the point that toward the last, even the Apostolic succession would end. Eventually, however, the Church would be reborn and rise again to world prominence "in the sight of all doubters."

DANIEL, PROPHECY OF. The apocalypse or series of visions which constitute the prophetic portion of the Book of Daniel, is contained in the second half of the work, namely Chapters 7 through 12. It is quite distinct in both language and style from the first portion, which consists of a dramatic narrative, recording a variety of events that happened during the reigns of Nebuchadnezzar, Belchazzar, and Darius.

Daniel's prophetic dreams, which occur at different times, foretell important events to come relative to the rulers of the world, the advent and death of the Messiah, the restoration of the Jews to their homeland and the Resurrection at "the end of days."

In both language and content, the apocalypse of Daniel anticipates the revelations of St. John, to which it is linked by many Christian expositors, particularly those of the Millenarian school.

There has been and continues to be considerable controversy surrounding the authorship and date of the

Book of Daniel. Some scholars say the work was written sometime early in the sixth century B.C., by a Jewish prophet named Daniel who was carried away captive to Babylon at an early age. There, as related in the
first half of the book bearing his name, he in time
became the first minister at the court of Babylon, after
he had shown great skill in interpreting the dreams of
Nebuchadnezzar.

Josephus, the renowned Jewish historian of the first
century A.D., refers to Daniel as one of the greatest
prophets, and asserts that he not only gave generalized
predictions of future events, but pinpointed the exact
time of their occurrence.

It was this latter fact—the striking coincidence of
Daniel's forecasts and their fulfillment—that led
Porphyry, a third-century adversary of Christianity, to
allege that they must have been written after the happenings which they describe had already taken place.

He further affirmed that Daniel was not the true
author of the prophecies, but that they must have been
written by some person who lived in Judea in the time
of Antiochus Epiphanes.

A number of liberal exegetes and historians of our
time have likewise tried to show that the work is of a
later date (perhaps as late as the second century B.C.)
thus discrediting its prophetic validity.

The Jewish canon, which was finalized in A.D. 90,
does not place Daniel among those books forming part
of the Hebrew Law or the Prophets, but in the division
known as the *Hagiographa*.

Some commentators have attributed this downgrad-
ing, so to speak, of Daniel as a prophet to the fact that
early Christians, including both Jesus and his disciples,
pointed to his predictions as presaging Christ as the
Messiah.

The first-century Jewish sect of Qumran, sometimes

identified as the Essenes, evidently esteemed the Book of Daniel. One of the Dead Sea Scrolls was found to be the earliest known copy, may date no more than one or two centuries from the original.

DA TERNI, FRA GEORGIO MARIA.   A 20th-century Capuchin monk and visionary of Perugia, Italy. Among his numerous prophecies concerning the immediate future is the following:

> "All the prophecies of the Gospels, the saints and the martyrs amply confirm that the present generation is that which will witness the end of the world. In 1972, Paul VI ascended the Papal throne, thus concretizing the schism dividing the Church.
> "The Red flag will flutter over the Vatican. God's punishment on Rome will be announced by an earthquake much stronger than that at Golgotha."

It should be noted that Fra Georgio's prediction of Paul VI's death as the result of a conspiracy in 1973 did not come to pass.

DAVIS, ANDREW JACKSON (1826–1910).   A prophet, clairvoyant and spiritualist, Jackson was born in Poughkeepsie, New York, in 1826. His career as a psychic began when he was about 18 years of age, after he had witnessed some experiments in Mesmerism.

He soon developed remarkable powers of clairvoyance and in 1847 published a volume of discourse entitled *The Principles of Nature*, which he had dictated during the trance state.

Davis also launched a periodical called the *Univercoelum*, devoted to reports and discussions of trance phenomena. The publication continued until 1849, and established Davis and his group as the leading psychic researchers of the day.

In 1848, the phenomena that would be known as spiritualism first began (or were first reported) when strange knockings were heard in the presence of the three Fox sisters in their home in Hydesville, New York. These raps were found to be a form of communication with a murdered peddler of the area.

As the spiritualist movement grew, Davis and his followers allied themselves with it, and contributed to the growing literature on the subject.

Davis defined his mission, which he said was revealed to him by Galen, the ancient Greek physician, and by Emanuel Swedenborg, the Swedish mystic, as the prophesying of a new dispensation upon earth.

In his *Penetralia*, Davis describes in amazing detail the motor car, airplane and other inventions, which were unknown in his day.

DEBORAH (c. 1125 B.C.).   A prophetess, wife of Lepidoth, assumed to be the writer who composed the *Song of Deborah*, a triumphal ode and one of the oldest poems in the Old Testament.

Although women were excluded from the religious hierarchy of ancient Israel, Deborah was held in such high regard that she was made the fourth judge of Israel, the only woman who ever filled that important office.

None of her prophecies, which probably concerned the immediate future of the Hebrews, has been preserved.

DELPHI.   Site of the famous oracle of Apollo on the southern slope of Mt. Parnassus in Greece. Here, for a thousand years, priestesses called Pythia delivered prophecies and answered the queries of petitioners while in a state of ecstasy.

During the early history of the oracle, the Pythia was a young virgin, but in later times the prophetess was an older woman, although still attired as a maiden.

In preparation for delivering her prophecy, the Pythia chewed a leaf of the sacred bay tree and drank from waters of a holy fountain called Cassotis, which flowed through the inner shrine. Then she seated herself upon a tall tripod in a subterranean cavern, the Adyton, and entered a trance.

There is no scientific evidence to support the popular notion that the tripod stood above a fissure in the earth, from which issued vapors which induced a state of altered consciousness in the prophetess.

The messages given by the Pythia were usually ambiguous and vague; at times, they consisted of little more than indistinct murmurs.

The meaning of these utterances had to be determined by priest-interpreters attached to the temple as intermediaries between the Pythia and their petitioners.

These holy men were usually from aristocratic families, and their office was a hereditary one which was passed down from one generation to another.

The Delphic Oracle's great renown began slowly to decline in the 5th century B.C., partly as a result of attacks by prominent public figures such as Euripides, the Greek dramatist.

By the time the Roman emperor Julian in the 4th century A.D. sent Oribasius to Delphi to restore the temples and sacred precincts, the Pythia's power of prophecy had been completely lost.

DIES IRAE (Day of Wrath).   A prophetic hymn embodying the intense emotions of medieval Christians as they contemplated "that tremendous day" when the heavens will pass away and the earth be dissolved in fervent heat.

For its power and majesty, the original Latin version of the hymn has been compared to the *Te Deum*.

Authorship of the work is ascribed by most scholars to Thomas de Celano, an Italian friar who was a follower of Francis of Assisi.

Melancthon W. Stryker, who made one of the more than one hundred translations of *Dies Irae*, says of it that "it remains the profoundest voice of guilty man fronting the cataclysms of eternal judgment. . . It flashes with forelight of the splendors and terrors of that last ordeal and gathers all hearts and all issues to face the focal day of earth's 'strange, eventful history.' "

DIXON, JEANE (1918–).   Well-known prophetess, astrologer and crystal gazer of Washington, D.C., whose predictions have been widely circulated in the popular press, both at home and abroad.

She was born in Wisconsin, the daughter of German immigrants Frank Pinckert and Emma von Graffee.

The family moved to California while Jeane was still a small child, and it was there that she reports having met a gypsy fortune-teller who found signs of the girl's psychic gifts while reading her palms.

The gypsy gave Jeane a crystal ball, telling her: "You will be able to meditate on this and see wonderful things in it, for the marking on your hands are those of a mystic."

Although she was reared in the Catholic faith, and still practices that religion, Mrs. Dixon seems able to reconcile her occult art with her orthodox beliefs. On occasion she even carries her crystal ball into church, along with her rosary.

In one instance of the kind, a revelation came to her

"while she was kneeling at prayer in St. Matthew's Cathedral, and holding in her hands a crystal ball." It was then she learned the contents of the as yet unreleased final message of Fatima. The incident is recounted in Ruth Montgomery's biography of Mrs. Dixon, *A Gift of Prophecy*:

> "Suddenly the very air seemed rarefied. A glorious light shown again from the dome of the cathedral, and before me stood the Holy Mother. She was draped in purplish blue and surrounded by gold and white rays which formed a halo of light around her entire person.
>
> "In a cloudlike formation to the right and just above her I read the word 'Fatima' and sensed that the long-secret prophecy of Fatima was to be revealed to me. I saw the throne of the Pope, but it was empty. Off to one side, I was shown a Pope with blood running down his face and dripping over his left shoulder. Green leaves of knowledge showered down from above, expanding as they fell. I saw hands reaching out for the throne, but no one sat in it, so I realized that within this century a Pope will be bodily harmed. When this occurs, the head of the Church will thereafter have a different insignia than that of the Pope. Because the unearthly light continued to shine so brightly on the papal throne, I knew that power would still be there but that it would not rest in the person of a Pope. Instead, the Catholic Church would blaze the trail for all peoples of every religion to discover the meaning of the Almighty Power; to grow in wisdom and knowledge. This I feel sure, was the prophecy of Fatima."

Among the numerous accurate predictions claimed for Mrs. Dixon in the past have been the assassinations of Mahatma Gandhi, John and Robert Kennedy, Martin Luther King; the suicide of Marilyn Monroe; the accidental death of UN Secretary General Dag Hammarskjold in a plane crash; the surprise election landslide for Eisenhower; and the partition of India.

There have likewise been many instances in which the Washington seeress has shot wide of the mark. These include her predictions that Russia would be the first nation to put a man on the moon; that Richard M. Nixon had "excellent vibes" for the good of America, and would serve his country well; that a tragic wave of suicide would engulf America; that great natural disasters would occur in the spring and early summer of 1977; that the President would "forge ahead with the controversial B-1 bomber; and—back in 1958—that Red China would plunge the world into war over Quemoy and Matsu.

> "When a psychic vision is not fulfilled as expected," explained Mrs. Dixon, "it is not because what has been shown is not correct; it is because I have not interpreted the symbols correctly."

Some of Mrs. Dixon's more important predictions for the future are:

1. In the mid-80s a comet (she may have meant meteor) will strike the earth, producing earthquakes and giant tidal waves.

2. A serious schism will split the Catholic church in matters of dogma and principle.

3. There will be germ warfare, which will be costly both in loss of lives and destruction of crops.

4. In the 1980s, a woman will be elected President of the United States.

5. Development of a new kind of propulsion, employ-

ing magnetic and cosmic forces, will enable U.S. astronauts to travel to distant planets.

6. During the present century, one pope will suffer bodily harm and another will be assassinated. The assassination will be the final blow to the Holy See.

7. In the year 2025, Red China will invade and conquer a large part of Russia's northern area and then continue on into Finland, Norway, Sweden and Denmark, stopping at the German border.

8. A great peace movement will follow world disarmament talks, but while peace seems to be on everyone's mind in the West, sudden destruction and war will occur in 1999.

DREAMS, PROPHETIC.   Perhaps the oldest form of prophecy or revelation of coming events is that of the precognitive dream.

Scholars are agreed that the art of foretelling the future probably originated in Babylon more than 5,000 years ago; and the earliest prophecies known to us are dream interpretations.

The Egyptions were ardent believers in prophetic dreams and had certain priests who specialized in dream interpretation.

Among the ancient Hebrews, too, God spoke to his people "by dreams and visions of the night." The scriptures are full of instances in which God revealed future events to His prophets through the medium of dreams.

"Prophecy," declared Maimonides, the great Jewish philosopher of the Middle Ages, "is, in truth and reality, an emanation sent forth by the Divine Being through the medium of the active intellect, in the first instance to man's rational faculty, and then to his imaginative faculty.

"The principal and highest function is performed when the senses are at rest and pause in their action, for then it receives, to some extent, divine inspiration in the measure as it is predisposed for this influence. This is the nature of those dreams which prove true, and also of prophecy, the difference being one of quantity, not of quality."

In his celebrated work, the *Summa Theologica*, St. Thomas Aquinas expressed the view that divination by dreams was permissible to faithful believers. "We read of holy men interpreting dreams," he wrote, "as Joseph interpreted the dreams of Pharaoh's butler and of his chief baker (Gen. 50:8) and the dreams of Pharaoh (Gen. 51:15); and Daniel interpreted the dreams of the King of Babylon (Dan. 2:26, 4:5). Therefore, divination by dreams is not unlawful."

In more recent times, various theories have been put forward to account for the prophetic content of dreams. One of these is that of the "eternal present," partially hinted at in H. G. Welles' work, *The Time Machine*, and fully formulated by the British writer J. W. Brodie-Innes:

"According to the theory, every dream is a partial consciousness of some scenes or events in this eternal present, events, that is, which may be present, or future. Just as we look at a landscape from a hilltop during a walk, it may be that we look at what we have passed, or at the path we intend to traverse, we see just what is before our eyes according to the direction in which they are turned. And because these events are often in the past, some have (rather rashly) concluded that every dream is merely a 'mix-up' of memories.

Those who dream much and who take the trouble to record and analyze their dreams, know that this is not so. Sometimes they may be able to trace past scenes, often hopelessly tangled up; suggesting that the brain has been conscious of many scenes, and been unable to classify and arrange them, and has simply presented to the waking consciousness a number of unrelated images, mixed in utter confusion. This will account for the confused dreams, said sometimes to be caused by indigestion or intoxication. They are not caused thereby, for a physical state cannot cause mental images, but the physical state may prevent the brain from co-ordinating the images it has received, and this may well account for the confusion. Even as it may account for the confusion of sight of well-known objects, the double vision of intoxication, for instance.

"But there come also dreams of the clear and healthy brain, picturing scenes of the past in definite and logical sequence, or other dreams of unknown scenes, which may be in the future, such as the clear pictures of places which perhaps we shall at some future time visit and identify, or scenes, as that recorded by M. Maeterlinck, which we shall some day experience and verify. Possibly we may thus be conscious of scenes that will never be part of our own lives, but it may be of the lives of others, and here we see the rationale of prophetic dreams concerning other people, of which there are some very clear recorded instances."

The most important theorist of precognitive dreams, however, was anything but a dreamer. He was John

William Dunne (q.v.) a British aeronautical engineer and physicist.

Dunne rejected the idea that prophetic dreams were the result of clairvoyance or some psychic gift possessed by the dreamer. Instead, he approached the whole subject in a scientific spirit which, after a series of experiments, led him to propound a new theory of time, called *serialism*.

Dunne's first book, *An Experiment With Time*, published in 1927, tells how he discovered what he terms "the displacement in time" that occurred in a number of dreams he recorded over a period of years.

Such a displacement, he maintained, resulted in the intermingling of images of both the past and future during the dream state. Moreover, he affirmed that everybody, not just mystics or seers, experiences these dreams, but that they are usually forgotten upon waking from sleep. "Nine-tenths of all dreams are completely forgotten within five seconds of waking," he wrote, "and the few which survive rarely outlast the operation of shaving. Even a dream which has been recalled and mentally noted is generally forgotten by the afternoon. Add to this the before-mentioned partial mental ban upon the requisite association; add to that an unconscious, matter-of-fact assumption of impossibility; and it becomes quite probable that it would be only a few of the more striking, more detailed and (possibly) more emotional incidents which would ever be noticed at all."

Dunne urges his readers to try for themselves the kind of dream experiments he conducted at various times and under a variety of circumstances. He gives the following instructions:

Keep a pencil and notebook under your pillow every night. Immediately upon waking and before opening your eyes, try to recall as much as possible of the rapidly vanishing dream of which you are still aware. If you can remember only a single incident of the dream, concentrate on that incident and try to recover its details.

> "As a rule, a single incident is all that you can re-call, and this appears so dim and small and iso-lated that you doubt the value of noting it down. Do not, however, attempt to remember anything more, but *fix your attention on that single inci-dent, and try to remember its details*. Like a flash, a large section of the dream in which that incident occurred, comes back. What is more important, however, is that, with that section there usually comes into view an isolated incident from a previous dream. Get hold of as many of these isolated incidents as you can, neglecting tempo-rarily the rest of the dreams of which they formed a part. Then jot down these incidents in your notebook as shortly as possible—a word or two for each should suffice.
> "Now take incident number one. Concentrate upon it until you have recovered part of the dream story associated therewith, and write down the briefest possible outline of that story. Do the same in turn with the other incidents you have noted. Finally, take the abbreviated record thus made and write it out in full. Note *details*, as many as possible. *Be specially careful to do this wherever the incident is one which, if it were to happen in real life, would seem unusual; for it is in connec-tion with events of this kind that your evidence is most likely to be obtained.*
> "Until you have completed your record, do not allow yourself to think of anything else.

"Do not attempt merely to remember. Write the dream down. Waking in the middle of the night, I have several times carefully memorized my preceding dreams. But, no matter how certain I have been that those memories were firmly fixed, I have never found one shred of them remaining in the morning. Even dreams which I have memorized just before getting up, and rememorized while dressing, have nearly always vanished by the end of breakfast.

"It will be impossible, of course, for you to write down *all* the details. To describe the appearance of a single dream-character completely would keep you busy for ten minutes. But write down the general detail, and *all uncommon detail*."

Dunne suggests that the worst time to choose for the experiment would be the period when you are leading a dull or routine life, with one day exactly like the last. He found that a visit to the theater or the cinema was a useful auxiliary to the experiment. (Dunne was writing before the advent of television in every living-room.)

He reminds his readers to guard against false interpretations. The dreaming mind, he observes, is very accomplished at giving false interpretations to everything it perceives. For that reason, your record of the dream should describe the *facts*, that is, the actual appearance of what is seen and the interpretation given to that appearance at the time.

Another difficulty which requires careful attention is that the waking mind refuses to accept the association between the dream and the subsequent event foreseen in it.

For the waking mind, "this association is the *wrong way round*, and no sooner does it make itself perceived than it is instantly rejected." Dunne adds that even when one is confronted with the indisputable evidence of the written record, one jumps at any excuse to avoid recognition.

Finally, Dunne recommends that at the end of each day of the experiment, you read your records over from the beginning.

DRUIDS. Celtic prophets, priests and teachers of pre-Roman Gaul and of the British Isles.

The most complete account of the Gallic Druids of antiquity is that of Julius Caesar, who relied for his information upon Divitiacus, a druidic noble of Aedui, which was a powerful Celtic nation with which the Romans had formed a close alliance.

Being a Roman, however, Caesar dwells at length upon the political and judicial functions of the Druids, without telling us a great deal about their most important office—that of prophecy or interpreting the will of the gods. It was, in fact, because they were so highly valued by their fellow men as seers that they were made judges and lawgivers.

A fourth-century work entitled *The Druidess*, by an anonymous author, says that the priestly office descended from father to son, and that even daughters took part in certain religious rites.

> "On the island of Saina," the account informs us, "these Druidesses formed a society which became famous throughout Gaul; and the sanctuary was held in such reverence by all the people that no one ventured to approach it.
> "When pious Gauls wished to consult the oracle, then came the priestesses to the coast and communicated to them the commands or will of the

gods, which was always received with the greatest gratitude and submission."

The same chronicle states that the Druidic oracle at
Toulouse ceased when Christianity was introduced
there by St. Saturinus.

Another oracle, dedicated to Apollo or Belanus,
flourished at Polignac in pre-Christian times.

A famous Druid temple on the Cornish coast of
England was served by nine virgins who took upon
themselves perpetual vows of chastity and who were
looked upon as interpreters of the gods. They were
believed to have power over tempests, which they
could call forth or allay at their pleasure.

The Irish Druids were also magicians as well as
prophets. The *vatis*, who were professional diviners,
practiced their art well into the Middle Ages, with the
consent and often the protection of the Christian priest-
hood. St. Patrick regarded them as quasi-priests.

The Celtic prophets received their revelations from
the wind, blowing through certain large trees. This
was one of the traditional methods of precognition
used by the Druids. St. Martin, the bishop of Tours,
and famous fourth-century exorcist, had a giant pine
felled because it was being used by a Druidic cult as a
means of foretelling the future.

DUNNE, JOHN WILLIAM (1875–1949).   Time theorist, aeronautical engineer, and physicist, was born in
1875, the son of General Sir John Hart Dunne. One of
England's earliest pilots and aircraft designers, in 1904
he invented the tailess type of aerofoil which still bears
his name. Three years later, he designed and built
Britain's first military aircraft.

During World War I, Dunne served as a Brigade

musketry instructor. British novelist J. B. Priestley, who was acquainted with both the man and his work, describes Dunne as a realist whose deep interest in metaphysics and time theory was based upon empirical investigation.

> "He had no secret love—as many of us have—of the miraculous. He had not been visited by any mystical revelations. . . . He was a hard-headed, military engineering type, whose hobby was not fantastic speculation and juggling with ideas, but fly-fishing."

A few writers have disputed this description of Dunne as being the complete man. After the publication of a posthumous work, *Intrusions?* (London, 1955), a German author even went so far as to characterize Dunne as having been secretly "a theosophical visionary—a new Swedenborg, in fact."

To support this extreme view, the writer—Prof. Richard Lewinsohn—pointed out that Dunne had repeatedly dreamt of an angel, which appeared to show him the path to true knowledge, and that he frequently heard mysterious voices.

Both these biographical assessments are probably accurate. Priestley's must be considered the more reliable, however, since he had personal contact with Dunne.

In any case, his work has to be judged on its own merits; and so considered, it undoubtedly represents an original and important contribution to the scientific study of precognition and time.

(For further information on Dunne's theory and method of experimentation, see article under *Dreams, Prophetic*.)

An ancient depiction of Babylonians prophesying by astrology, making it one of the earliest sciences and structured bodies of knowledge known to man.

A drawing of the "Apocalyptic Zodiac" wherein the figure of man is surrounded by the twelve symbols of the zodiac.

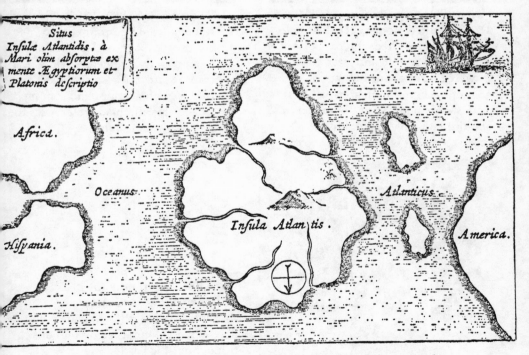

The subject of legend and mystery for centuries, Atlantis, "The Lost Continent," continues to this day to mystify and fascinate. Shown above is Kircher's map of Atlantis (c. 1644). Arrow indicates north.

Helena Petrovna Blavatsky (1831–1891), a noted modern occultist and founder of the Theosophical Society, was born in Russia and later travelled throughout the world gaining recognition in spiritualist circles. She made accurate predictions about the fate of "materialistic science" which were proven correct.

Edgar Cayce (1887–1945), the world famous sleeping prophet who accurately diagnosed medical ills and prescribed remedies while in a trance state, but also spoke of future earth changes and coming cataclysms and made references to Atlantis and its culture.

Jeane Dixon, certainly the best known modern-day seeress and astrologer, who writes a syndicated newspaper column read by millions throughout the world. She correctly predicted the assassinations of both Kennedys as well as Martin Luther King.

The illustration above depicts Druid worship in ancient Gaul.
The Druids were Celtic prophets, priests and teachers
of pre-Roman Gaul and of the British Isles.

The visionary and stigmatic Ann Catherine Emmerich, to whom appeared the Holy Virgin and m angels from the time of her early childhood. By the age of 24, she began to experience the phenome of stigmata.

Our Lady of Fatima depicted in white marble at the shrine where the vision was first seen in 1917.

L. Ron Hubbard, founder of the Church of Scientology. The word is derived from the Latin *scio*, meaning "to know" and the Greek *logos* or word, meaning the outward form by which the inward thought is expressed.

EGYPT. In ancient Egypt, prophecy—which meant revelation of the divine will with respect to future events —most often took the form of dream interpretation. This art, which the Egyptians received from Babylonia, was widely practiced on both the priestly and secular levels of society.

Dreams of the Pharaohs were deemed most important of all because the rulers were sons of the Sun (Ra), the light and life of all creation. Too, the fate of the people was directly involved with that of the king.

The most famous Pharaoh's dream on record is, of course, that related in the Bible concerning the seven fat and seven lean years, so ably interpreted by Joseph.

The dream of another Pharaoh is recorded on a granite monument, known as the *Stele of the Dream*. Its hieroglyphics relate how Pharaoh Amen-meri Nut dreamed that he beheld on either side of him a serpent. The prophet-priest construed this to mean that the king would conquer the lands to the north and south of his kingdom. The account goes on to say that the prophecy came true: Amen-meri Nut recaptured first Ethiopia and then Memphis.

During the old and middle kingdoms, a special order of priestesses—women from important families—were known as prophetesses and delivered oracular messages from the temples of Hathor and Neith.

Egyptian experts in the art of prophetic dreams offered those who consulted them not only an interpretation of dreams, but magic formulae for inducing such dreams. A papyrus preserved in the British museum gives the following directions for producing fatidic dreams:

> "Take a clean linen bag and write upon it the names given below. Fold it up and make it into a lamp wick, and set it alight, pouring pure oil over it. The words to be written are these: 'Armiuth, Lailamchouch, Arsenophrephren, Phtha, Archentechtha.' Then in the evening, when you are going to bed, which you must do without touching food, do thus: Approach the lamp and repeat seven times the formula given below: then extinguish it and lie down to sleep. The formula is this: 'Sachmu—apaema Ligotereench: the Aeon, the Thunderer, thou that hast swallowed the snake and dost exhaust the moon, and dost raise up the orb of the sun in his season, Chthetho is the name; I require, O lords of the gods, Seth, Cherps, give me the information that I desire.' "

Astrology also had its place in Egyptian prophecy, especially in the time of the later Pharaohs. The two principal centers of astrological prediction were Heliopolis and Alexandria. The Roman emperor Trajan, shortly before his death, sent an envoy to the oracle at Heliopolis to obtain a reading of the future. He had just put down a serious uprising in the north, and the Parthians were threatening to counter-attack the Roman forces. All over the empire, there were other signs of trouble.

In reply to Trajan's query, the oracle at Heliopolis sent the emperor without further comment a broken sarmentum plant—a slender, prostrate runner. Soon afterward, on his way back to Rome, Trajan died in Cilicia.

There were also pyramid prophets who officiated at daily rites in the temples that were always erected before the royal pyramids. Their prophecies and rituals have largely been lost.

ELIZABETH OF SCHONAU (1129–1164).   Benedictine nun and prophetess, was born in the Rhineland in 1129. She entered the Benedictine order when she was only 12, and was professed when she was 18.

Five years after taking the veil, Elizabeth began to experience prodigious visions, which her brother, Egbert, helped her to record in detail. These contained denunciations of the clergy and warnings of the calamities and retribution awaiting the wicked, much after the manner of Hildegarde's famous work, *Scivias*.

A number of Elizabeth's visions (apparently stimulated by the opening of an old Roman burial ground in Cologne) added new dimensions to the already bizarre legend of St. Ursula and her legion of sacred virgins.

The nun's contemporaries all testify to her sincerity and piety; and her writings exercised a deep influence over the people of medieval Europe, even though they were never officially approved by the Church.

EMMERICH, ANNA CATHERINE (1774–1824). Visionary and stigmatic, was born at Flamske, a village near Coesfeld, Germany, on September 8, 1774.

The daughter of peasants, her early years were spent in poverty and hard labor in the fields. From her childhood, she experienced extraordinary visions in which the Holy Virgin and many of the saints appeared to her and, according to her account, gave her flower garlands which she brought to the church in honor of their respective festivals.

She began to show the first signs of stigmata when she was 24 years of age. She describes the experience in these words:

> "About four years previous to my admittance into the convent, consequently in 1798, it happened that I was in the Jesuits' Church at Coesfeld at about twelve o'clock in the day, kneeling before a crucifix and absorbed in meditation, when all of a sudden I felt a strong but pleasant heat in my head, and I saw my Divine Spouse under the form of a young man clothed with light, come towards me from the altar, where the Blessed Sacrament was preserved in the tabernacle. In his left hand he held a crown of flowers; in his hight hand a crown of thorns; and he bade me choose which I would have. I chose the crown of thorns; he placed it on my head, and I pressed it down with both hands. Then he disappeared, and I returned to myself, feeling, however, violent pain about my head. I was obliged to leave the church, which was going to be closed. One of my companions was kneeling by my side, and as I thought she might have seen what happened to me, I asked her when we got home whether there was not a wound on my forehead, and spoke to her in general terms of my vision, and of the violent pain which had followed it. She could see nothing out-

wardly, but was not astonished at what I told her because she knew that I was sometimes in an extraordinary state, without her being able to understand the cause. The next day my forehead and temples were very much swelled, and I suffered terribly. The pain and swelling often returned and sometimes lasted whole days and nights. I did not remark that there was blood on my head until my companions told me I had better put on a clean cap, because mine was covered with red spots. I let them think whatever they liked about it, only taking care to arrange my head-dress so as to hide the blood which flowed from my head, and I continued to observe the same precaution ever after I entered the convent, where only one person perceived the blood, and she never betrayed my secret."

Subsequently, Anna Catherine experienced stigmatic wounds in her hands and on her side and feet.

When the king of Westphalia suppressed the Augustinian order to which Anna Catherine belonged, and closed the convent in December 1811, the visionary nun, poor and chronically ill, remained at the shuttered convent, attended by a kindhearted former servant of the institution. The following year, she moved into a wretched little room of a private home belonging to an impoverished widow.

There her intercourse with the invisible world increased, and she began to manifest further stigmata. Abbe de Cazales says of her that:

"On the 28th of August, the feast of St. Augustine, the patron of her order, as she was making this prayer in bed, ravished in ecstasy and her arms stretched forth, she beheld a young man approach her, surrounded with light. It was under this form that her Divine Spouse usually appeared to her, and he now made upon her body with his right hand the mark of a common cross. From this time, there was a mark like a cross on her bosom, consisting of two bands crossed, about three inches long and one wide. Later the skin often rose in blisters on this place, as if from a burn, and when these blisters burst, a colourless liquid issued from them, sometimes in such quantities as to soak through several sheets. She was long without perceiving what the case really was, and only thought that she was in a strong perspiration. The particular meaning of this mark has never been known.

"Some weeks later, when making the same prayer, she fell into an ecstasy, and beheld the same apparition, which presented her with a little cross of the shape described in her accounts of the Passion. She eagerly received and fervently pressed it to her bosom, and then returned it. She said that this cross was soft and white as wax, but she was not at first aware that it had made an external mark upon her bosom. A short time after, having gone with her landlady's little girl to visit an old hermitage near Dulmen, she all of a sudden fell into an ecstasy, fainted away, and on her recovery was taken home by a poor peasant woman. The sharp pain which she felt in her chest continued to increase, and she saw that there was what looked like a cross, about three inches in length, pressed tightly upon her breastbone, and looking red through the skin."

Later, a second and smaller cross appeared on top of the first, so that together they formed a double forked cross.

During the last five years of Anna Catherine's life, Clemens Brentano, a poet and prominent literary figure of the day, stayed by her side and made day-to-day transcriptions of her visions. These included a lengthy account of the Crucifixion, starting with the Last Supper and concluding with the Resurrection.

In that work, entitled *The Dolorous Passion of Our Lord Jesus Christ*, she declares that Lucifer will be unchained and released from the infernal pit "fifty or sixty years before the year of Christ 2000."

> "But a certain number of demons are to be set loose much earlier than Lucifer, in order to tempt men and to serve as instruments of divine vengeance."

ENGLAND IN PROPHECY. Predictions regarding the future of Great Britain—indeed, of most nations— are traditionally dark. Some seers have prophesied that the British Isles will sink beneath the sea or be overwhelmed by a vast tidal wave; others that the island nation will slowly fade away, politically and economically speaking. Nostradamus foresees Britain united with the U.S. in a political venture, setting up a dictator who in the end will betray both nations. (X:66)

In recent times, several prophets have predicted the end of the British monarchy. For example, Hades, the French astrologer, writes that "before the end of the century, the monarchy will be abolished in England. Such is the brutal and dramatic fact forecast by the stars."

He foreshadows a succession of difficult years for the country, and a series of misfortunes affecting the royal family.

From 1984 onward, a number of crises will occur, "culminating at the enigmatic date of 1999. Why do I call that date enigmatic? Because it appears that at that point in time, the Occident will no longer exist. Powerful and sudden upheavals are shaping up."

After studying the prophecies of soothsayers, both ancient and modern, Josane Charpentier also pictures troubled times ahead for Britain,

> "Queen Elizabeth II is, without doubt, the last English sovereign." Then, in a footnote, the writer points out that "in Westminster Abbey, only one place remains in the royal burial crypt. Moreover, it is generally believed that Prince Charles, according to his horoscope, has not the slightest possibility of being crowned king."

This does not mean that there will be a revolution in Britain. Rather, Charles will simply ask, very amiably, that he be permitted to abdicate. When he does, the monarchy will end. This could occur before 1985.

Alan Vaughan, basing his forecast upon a theory of ancient archetypal patterns, sees Britain as having reached the same point in her history as Athens experienced when it lost its colonies, but retained its wisdom as "the university of the world." He asks: will some modern British philosopher take the role as Aristotle to some future world conqueror comparable to Alexander the Great?

EZEKIEL (6th century B.C.).   Hebrew priest and prophet, was the son of Buzi, of the clan of Zadok. He was one of the captives who, along with King Jehoiachim, were deported to Babylon by Nebuchadnezzar after the fall of Jerusalem in 597 B.C.

Ezekiel was a member of the exile community which was settled at Tel-abib near the river Chebar, which flows into the Euphrates about 200 miles north of Babylon.

His prophetic ministry began in 592, about five years after he began his exile in Babylonia.

What is known factually of the events of his life is based chiefly upon what he records in his book. However, much concerning the prophet's personality and religious outlook can be inferred from the bold, vehement style of his writings. His great erudition and genius, his beautiful metaphors, and the sublimity of his conceptions make his work incomparable in prophetic literature.

Ezekiel had a divine gift, marked by a contemplative temperament and the ability to enter a trance state in which he was transported through time and space to witness events in both the immediate and the remote future.

The difficulty in interpreting some of his symbolic passages led the authorities of ancient Israel to forbid Jews under the age of 30 to read his work.

The *Book of Ezekiel* treats of the following principal subjects: the prophet's divine call to prophesy; his prediction of the imminent fall of Jerusalem; a diatribe against the Ammonites, Moabites, Edomites, and Philistines; the downfall of Tyre and Egypt; prophecies foretelling the restoration of Israel "in the latter days," and a vision of the final war of mankind, when Gog, a ruler from the land of Magog, leads a vast army from various nations in an unsuccessful attack on God's people.

Several of the last chapters of the book bear a marked resemblance, in tone and content, to St. John's Apocalypse. Contemporary students of Bible prophecy—especially the millenarists—consider the visions of Ezekiel as an integral part of the main body of revealed truth relating to the final destiny of man and his world, as also foreshadowed in the other Hebrew prophets and by John in the New Testament.

Some modern expositors have expressed the belief that the curious wheels described in Ezekiel's opening vision were in fact flying saucers or space ships such as those reported so often in the sightings of recent years.

After telling how he saw four strange, humanoid creatures whose appearance was "as if fire from burning coals or torches were darting to and fro among them," the prophet proceeds to picture the weird vehicles controlled by them:

> "As I looked at the living creatures, I saw wheels on the ground, one beside each of the four. The wheels sparkled like topaz, and they were all alike: in form and working they were like a wheel inside a wheel, and when they moved in any of the four directions they never swerved in their course. All four had hubs and each hub had a projection which had the power of sight, and the rims of the wheels were full of eyes all around. When the living creatures moved, the wheels moved beside them; when the creatures rose from the ground, the wheels rose; they moved in whatever direction the spirit would go; and the wheels rose together with them, for the spirit of the living creatures was in the wheels."

Ezekiel's vision of the valley of dry bones (Ezek. 37:1–14) has also become famous in exegetical literature.

Nothing is known about the last years of Ezekiel's life. The Pseudo-Epiphanius says in his work, *Lives of the Prophets*, that he was put to death by the leader of the exiled Hebrews because of his denunciation of that official's idolatry; but scholars view this account with some reservation.

FATIMA, PROPHECY OF.   During World War I, on
May 13, 1917, one of the most famous prophecies in
history was given to three shepherd children near the
small Portuguese village of Fatima.

On that day, the three children—Lucia, 10; Francisco,
9; and Giacinta, 7—said they saw "a beautiful lady
from heaven," brighter than the sun, standing upon a
cloud atop an evergreen tree.

Lucia, the oldest child, said the shining apparition
conversed with them for the space of several minutes.
She asked the children to meet her at the same spot on
the 13th day of each month until October, at which
time she would tell them who she was. Then she disappeared.

In the ensuing months, the children returned on the
dates promised, despite the skepticism of the people in
their village regarding their experience.

The apparition recurred six times between May 13
and October 13, 1917. As news of the strange event

spread, an increasing number of spectators accompanied the children to the scene of their tryst with the beautiful Lady. The crowds grew, from about 50 persons on June 13, to an estimated 50,000 at the final manifestation on October 13.

Only the children were able to see the Lady, although many others reported that they observed a bright cloud over the tree.

An influential group of unbelievers and political radicals strongly opposed the children's visits to the site of the apparition to "put an end to the nonsense" that was attracting such wide attention. On the appointed day in August the civil prefect of Outrem seized the children and spirited them away in hopes of eliciting from them an admission that the whole affair was a hoax. He kept them in custody for two days, submitting them to intense interrogation and threats. The children stuck to their story.

Although the three youngsters had been forcibly kept from their August 13 meeting, the Lady appeared to them six days later at Valinhos, not far from the original site of the apparition. She informed them that she would appear once more on October 13 and show them a miracle, as a sign to the people that the events were real.

On that date, a vast crowd gathered at Cova da Iria (the place of the apparition) and waited in a steady downpour of rain for the promised miracle to occur. Among them were a number of highly skeptical reporters who had already written articles derisive of the happenings.

The shining figure appeared to the children and told them she was Our Lady of the Rosary and imparted to them three messages or "secrets" regarding things to come.

The spectators could not see nor hear what was unfolding before them, but what happened next left most of them visibly shaken by the experience. Newspaper accounts at the time indicate clearly that even those journalists who had previously scoffed at reports of the occurrences had amended their views.

According to their eyewitness accounts, the rain suddenly stopped and the sun appeared, then seemed to rotate rapidly, and to plunge earthward, gyrating crazily.

Terrified, people dropped to their knees and prayed.

In a moment or two, the sun returned to its normal position. Then the phenomenon was repeated two more times.

Published accounts of the prodigy reported that the rain-soaked clothing of the crowd became dry during the sun's odd behavior.

Francisco and Jacinto died during the 1918–1919 influenza pandemic that swept Western Europe.

Lucia was taught to read and write, and later wrote down the prophecy or "secret" of Fatima.

There were three parts to the prophecy, two of which have been made public. The third was opened by Pope John XXIII in 1960, as directed by the Madonna at Fatima. But the message was never divulged to the world.

A source inside the Vatican reported that one day the Pope confided to a few friends how he had read the third secret of Fatima and that upon reading it, "he had trembled with fear and had almost fainted with horror."

In the first portions of the prophecy, Lucia related how the Virgin had spread her arms, and from her hands had projected a stream of light which penetrated the earth and became a sea of fire.

"In that sea were drowning demons and beings in

human form, charred and black, like hot coals. Carried into the air by the flames, they fell back again like sparks in a huge conflagration, without weight or equilibrium, emitting loud cries and screams of pain and desperation. It made one shake and tremble with fear.

"The demons could be distinguished from persons by their forms, which were horrible and loathsome—monstrous and unknown animal creatures, but translucent like coals of fire.

"This sight lasted but an instant, and we were grateful to the Heavenly Mother for having promised to take us to heaven. I think that had it not been so, we would have died of terror and fright.

"To beg succor, we lifted our eyes to Our Lady, who kindly and sadly told us:

" 'You have seen hell, where the unhappy souls of the wicked will go. In order to save them, the Lord wishes to establish in the world devotion to my immaculate heart. If you do what I tell you, many souls will be saved and there will be peace.' "

The second part of the prophecy foreshadowed World War II:

"The war [World War I] is coming to an end. But if people do not cease to offend the Lord, another and more terrible one will break out during the next pontificate. When you see the night lit up by a great, unknown light, know that it is a sign that God gives you that punishment of the world by another war, famine and persecution of the Church and of the Holy Father.

(This part of the Fatima prophecy was fulfilled on the night of January 25–26, 1938, between the hours of 9 and 11 P.M., when the skies of Western Europe were lighted by a strange light, identified as an extraordinary aurora borealis. In the Alps, the light was so brilliant that night postal employees worked without any kind of artificial light. Less than two months later, Hitler invaded Austria.)

> "In order to prevent this, I have come to intercede for the conversion of Russia and for Communion on the first sabbath of each month.
>
> "If you carry out my requests, Russia will be converted and there will be peace. If not, Russia will extend her errors [i.e. Communism] throughout the world, provoking wars and persecutions against the Church. Many good people will become martyrs. The Holy Father will suffer much. Several nations will be annihilated.
>
> "In the end, however, my Immaculate Heart will triumph; Russia will be converted and the world will enjoy a period of peace."

There has been much speculation about the contents of the third and final "secret" of Fatima, which the Pope apparently found to be too frightening to make public.

The educated guess of those who know most about the subject, is that the last message from Fatima was a warning of an end to the Papacy, and a final atomic war that will destroy the world, following the period of peace referred to in the preceding secret.

In what was most likely a political move to assuage the curiosity of the public, which was anxiously awaiting the concluding revelations on Our Lady of the Rosary, an alleged text of the document was published by the German *News Europa* on October 15, 1963. Until it is declared by the Holy See to be authentic, it should be received with a certain amount of caution. The published prophecy reads:

"Have no fear, little one. I am the Mother of God who speaks to you and asks you to publish the message I am going to give you to the whole world. You will find strong resistance while you do so. Listen well and pay attention to what I tell you.

"Men must be set on the right road once more. With suppliant humility, men must seek forgiveness for sins committed already and which will be committed. You wish me to give you a sign, so that everyone will accept My Words, which I am saying through you, to the human race. I have seen the Prodigy of the Sun and all believers, unbelievers, peasants, countrywomen, wise men, journalists, laics and priests all have seen it. And now I proclaim in my Name: A great punishment shall fall on the entire human race, not today and not tomorrow, but in the second half of the twentieth century! I have already revealed to the children Melania and Maximine at La Salette, and today I repeat it to you, for the human race has sinned and has trampled down the Gift which I have made. In no part of the world is life in order, Satan rules in the highest position, laying down how things should be done. He will effectually succeed in bringing his influence right up to the top of the Church; succeed in seducing the spirits of the great scientists who invent the arms which in ten minutes could easily wipe out all humanity. He will have under his power the rulers who govern the people and will help them to make an enormous quantity of these arms. And if humanity opposes me I shall be obliged to free the arm of My Son. Now I see that God will punish man with a severity that has not been used since the Flood.

"The time of times will come and everything will come to an end if humanity is not converted, and if things remain as they are now or get worse, or get very much worse the great and powerful men will perish just as will the small and weak.

"For the Church, too, the time of its greatest trial will come. Cardinals will oppose cardinals and bishops against bishops. Satan will march in their midst and there will be great changes at Rome. What is rotten will fall, never to rise again. The church will be darkened and the world will shake with terror. The time will come when no king, emperor, cardinal or bishop will await Him who will, however, come, but in order to punish according to the designs of my Father.

"A great war will break out in the second half of the twentieth century. Fire and smoke will fall from heaven, the waters of the oceans will become vapours, the scum will arise in a confused manner, and everything will sink down. Millions and millions of men will perish while this is going on and those who survive will envy the dead. The unexpected will follow in every part of the world, anxiety, pain and misery in every country. Have I seen it? The time is getting ever nearer and the abyss is getting wider without hope. The good will perish with the bad, the great with the small, the Heads of the Church with their faithful, and the rulers with their people. There will be death everywhere as a result of the mistakes of the unfeeling and the partisans of Satan, but when those who survive all these happenings are still alive, they will proclaim God again and His Glory, and will serve him as in the time when the world was not so perverted.

"Go, my little one and proclaim it. For that purpose I shall always be at your side to help you."

FERRER, VINCENT FR. (d. 1419):　A Spanish Dominican friar, mystic and master of the palace to Pope Benedict XIII. During the 15th century he was highly regarded as an inspired preacher who was called to prophesy the future.

A millenarian, he announced the great fact that the public advent of the Antichrist would occur in a few years, and urged his hearers to prepare for the severe struggle with satanic forces that was sure to follow. In a letter to Benedict XIII, he assured the Pontiff that he knew as a certainty that the Antichrist was already nine years old.

This "fact" had been revealed by demons who confessed it during the rite of exorcism.

FRANCE IN PROPHECY.　France figures prominently in most prophecies concerning the final wars of mankind, as well as the natural catastrophes that will accompany them.

The mystical *Centuries* of Nostradamus are filled with prognostications concerning French history, past and present. As for the future, interpreters of the 16th century prophet cite several quatrains in which, they say, Nostradamus predicts that during the latter part of this century, France will be weakened from within by Communists, thus preparing the way for an invasion of red forces composed of a red-Arab alliance. The enemies will attack from five directions at one time.

The Madonna of La Salette warned that there will be civil war in France—"blood will flow in the streets, Frenchman will fight Frenchman."

Hades, the French astrologer, has predicted that France will veer to the left politically, to be followed by an authoritarian government not too different in practice from the old monarchy.

"From that time on," he writes, "different political convulsions will provide an opportunity for the left, even the extreme left."

The total destruction of Paris toward the end of the present century has long been a favorite theme of many prophecies. More than thirty forecasts, ancient and contemporary, predict that Paris will perish in flames.

Caesar of Arles, like many who came before and after him, foresaw "the conquest, exploitation and devastation of the most illustrious and most famous capital and queen of all France."

One of the most extraordinary descriptions of that terrible event is contained in one of the last books written by the controversial French author Celine. He gives us his apocalyptic vision in these words:

"Twenty *quartiers* were sizzling! The Luxembourg was reduced to a rose! a burning rosebush! The Academie melted. . . beige. . . green. . . dripped down to the Quai, to the Seine. . . its cupola floats for a moment. . . turns over. . . sinks! Ah, and the Madeleine and Chamber of Deputies are flying away. . . swollen balloons. They rise a little. . . get their balance. . . pass by, all blue! red! white! explode!

"Other artifices follow! tracer bullets far away. . . with the most original trajectories. . . spirals. . . they look as if they were sewing the clouds. . . sewing them together. . . hemming them! . . . with blue! . . . mauve! canary yellow!"

Such a nightmarish vision does not seem so far-fetched when one remembers the blood-curdling, terse telegram sent by Hitler to the general he had ordered to put the torch to Paris during the last war:

"Is Paris burning?"

GARABANDAL, SAN SEBASTIAN DE. A village
of Spain about 67 miles from the port of Santander. In
June 1961, four Spanish children—Conchita, Maria Do-
lores, Jacinta, and Maria Cruz—reported seeing an apparition of the Virgin of Mt. Carmel in a grove of pines
at a site called Pini.

The manifestation occurred again on December 8,
1964, at which time the Virgin spoke to Conchita,
warning that great punishment awaited humanity if
the world's people did not repent of their sins and mend
their ways. She promised a public miracle at some future date, an event, she said, that would upset the
materialistic views of those who witnessed it, and
would convert many unbelievers.

In all, five apparitions occurred between June 1961
and December 1965.

Conchita said that during the appearance on January
1, 1965, the Virgin had revealed to her that a sign
visible throughout the world would precede the promised miracle.

"I cannot tell exactly what she said, as she ordered me not to do so. She did not tell me when it would happen and thus I do not know. Yes, I know that it will be visible all over the world; it will be the direct work of God, and will take place before the miracle. I do not know whether anyone will die. But my impression is that some will die."

Conchita said the Virgin had forbidden her to say what form the miracle would take or to forecast the exact day it would occur. "I can reveal the date only eight days before it happens. What I can say is that it will coincide with the feast-day of a holy martyr; that it will occur at 8:30 P.M. on a Thursday; that it will be visible to all the people who are in the village of Garabandal or the surrounding mountains; the sick who see it will be cured and the unbelievers will believe. It will be the greatest miracle that Jesus has ever performed in the world. There will be no doubt that it will come from God and that it will be for the benefit of humanity. A trace of the miracle will remain at Pini forever. It will be able to be filmed and to appear on television."

Conchita said the Virgin told her that humanity will be punished if people do not heed the warning given, and by the miracle. "If it comes," she said, "I know what form it will take because the Virgin has told me; but I cannot say. Furthermore, I have seen the punishment. Yes, I can assure you that it is worse than if one had fire both above and below one. I do not know how long it will be before God sends it after the miracle has been performed."

The obvious similarity of the Garabandal apparition and message to that of Fatima was further compounded eleven years later when a group of 40 British tourists visiting the site where the Virgin had appeared saw a "dancing sun" like that reported by observers at Cova da Iria in Portugal on October 13, 1917.

Father Alec Barilone, a Catholic priest of London, who accompanied the group, later declared unequivocally: "I definitely saw the sun spinning very fast—first clockwise, then counter-clockwise, surrounded by all sorts of colors. I believe it was a miraculous manifestation."

Mrs. Gwendoline Hurndall, a nurse at St. Joseph's Hospital in London, gave a more detailed account of the event in these words:

> "At about 6:45 one evening during our visit, we had gone to a clump of pines above the village to pray, when I heard cries of 'Look at the sun!' I looked up and found that I could look straight at the sun without sunglasses. Part of the outline of a cross was just vanishing from the sun as I looked up. Then the sun began to spin like a wheel, first one way and then the other. Then it jumped up and down like a yo-yo for a few minutes before starting to spin again.
>
> "While all this was happening, different colors were emerging and receding around it—pink, yellow, blue, gray. This went on for about half an hour. Then some of us decided to pray again, and just as we knelt, the sun divided itself into two parts. A central part stood forward from the rest and moved toward us like a huge host, a sacred communion wafer."

Other members of the group described similar experiences.

GILTHIER, RIDOLFO (17th century).   An Augustine monk and missionary who, in August 1675, had a prophetic vision which he committed to paper. The Latin text was discovered in 1855 in an ancient book kept in the Augustine Library of Rome. Some of the events prophesied by Gilthier have already come to pass; others are yet to appear. Among the latter are the following:

— A great military leader from the North will deploy a huge army that will overrun Europe and conquer the democratic countries, exterminating all who resist. The Arabs, too, will invade Europe, but when the Northern commander sees what ruin they leave in their wake, he will restrain them.

— A new Pontiff, summoned by a sign in heaven, will lead the faithful in simplicity of heart and knowledge of Christ. Then peace will return to the world.

For the most part, the prophecy is unoriginal and imitative of the *Centuries* of Nostradamus, by whom Gilthier was patently influenced.

HEERING, CHRISTIAN (b. 1710). Saxon missionary, clairvoyant, and fisherman. His revelations were recorded by his confessor, the Rev. Johann Gabriel Susse.

Heering received his revelations in the waking state. He saw figures and scenes, and heard voices. "I do not prophesy, nor do I direct," he once said. "I merely point out what the Lord ordered me to point out. And three times I have sworn that I should hold back nothing commanded by the Lord, out of fear for myself or for my family."

Heering's predictions were usually accurate, including a number of them that were filled with detailed descriptions of what would happen. He successfully forecast the invasion and defeat of Saxony by Frederick the Great two years before it occurred; the mutual assistance treaty between Louis XV of France and Maria Theresa of Austria, in alliance against Frederick; the Seven Years War; and other events which took place during his lifetime.

HERMANN, BROTHER (c. 1270 A.D.).   A monk resident in the monastery of Lehnin, in Brandenburg,
Prussia. Few details are known concerning his personal
life. His prophecies, written in a hundred rhyming hex-
ameters, were printed in 1723, or more than five hundred years after his death. They are concerned chiefly
with the future affairs of his own religious community,
and those of the house of Hohenzollern.

He predicted in detail the plundering of Brandenburg by robber barons, who would be defeated by a
strong emperor (Charles IV). Then he accurately foretold the rise of the Hohenzollerns, stating correctly that
the first prince of the line would gain recognition by
holding two castles. It happened as he had said, the
two castles being those of Nuremberg and Brandenburg.

HILDEGARDE,   SAINT   (1098–1179).   Visionary,
mystic, Abbess of Rupertsberg, near Bingen on the
Rhine. Although she is known as St. Hildegarde, she
was never canonized by the Church. She was born of
noble parents at Bockelheim, near Sponheim, Germany.

When she was eight years old, she entered the Benedictine cloister to begin formal education, and remained the rest of her life a member of that religious
community.

From her childhood onward, Hildegarde experienced
visions in which she said she could foresee future events
as though they were happening in the present. In later
life, she wrote:

> "I was only in my third year when I saw a heaven-
> ly light which made my soul tremble, but the
> impediments of infancy prevented me from
> bringing forth anything."

When she was 42 years old, the prophetess said an

interior voice ordered her to publish all that she had seen and heard. The result was an extensive collection of writings, which include prophecies, letters, a miracle play, homilies, medical treatises, and hymns. Her principal work, *Scivias*, alone contained 200 pages of fine print in a quarto volume that was divided into three books.

J. J. von Dollinger accurately observed that Hildegarde stands quite alone in the whole of Christian history. "No prophet has ever acquired so high a reputation; no saint has ever won such general acknowledgment, such unbounded reverence."

Above all else, Hildegarde was an apocalyptic prophetess in the awesome tradition of Ezekiel and John the Revealer. In her terror-filled visions, she heard voices that spoke in tones of thunder; saw shapes of mountainous size, and a blazing coruscation she called "the true, the divine, the living light."

Her revelations cover the passing of five epochs of world history, filled with human wickedness and the turning away from spiritual values, until the days of the end, when the earth will be consumed in a final cataclysm of fire, wind, and water.

Contemporary accounts of Hildegarde's life tell of many miraculous cures she effected, sometimes by a touch, sometimes at a distance by sending holy water to be applied to the sick person's lips or afflicted parts. She was highly regarded as an exorcist, being endowed by God, it was said, with the power of delivering persons possessed by demons.

In her writings, the holy nun has interesting passages that describe the manner in which people become possessed and how the evil spirit uses his victim.

"It is by means of spirits of the air," she explains, "that Satan holds intercourse with them; for the wickedness of men charges the atmosphere with a kind of spirits who, like swarms of flies or gnats, hover in innumerable hosts around the perverse."

In one vision, Hildegarde said, she saw a possessed person surrounded by a thick and hellish effluvia which, enveloping the whole sensible part of his rational being, prevented the spiritual part from exercising its free will.

"The soul, having thus lost the perfect use of its senses and of its proper faculties, uttered cries and performed actions which had no real meaning.

"Whilst I meditated upon what I saw, and sought to learn how and by what means the form (the *substance*) of the demon enters into man, I was answered and, in fact, I saw that the demon does not enter into man with his proper form, but covers and envelopes him with the shadow and effluvia of his darkness. For if the form of the demon entered into men, the bond which unites their members would at once be burst; it would be dispelled more quickly than chaff before the wind. For this reason, God does not permit the demon to enter within us in his form. But, penetrating our being with his darkness, as I have said, he throws us into a kind of rage or madness which causes us to say and do strange things. He vomits forth by our mouth, as from a window, blasphemies against God; affects our members from outside of them, though he is not really within us in his form. During this time, the human soul, as it were, deafened and stupefied, ignores what the flesh performs."

Like prophets of the Old Testament, Hildegarde fearlessly denounced high-ranking ecclesiastics of her day for the evil lives they led. Nor did she shrink from rebuking popes, kings, princes, and bishops when the spirit moved her to do so.

In her *Heptachronon*, she forecasts events that are to occur in the twentieth century:

> "It will come to pass at the close of the fifth epoch," she says, "that the clergy and the Church will be enveloped in the nets of a horrible schism and the greatest confusion, so that they shall be driven from the places which they inhabited. Even as from the days of its founder, the Catholic faith spread itself gradually and little by little until at length it shone forth in the splendor of justice and truth, so in those days of folly and weakness it will descend by degrees from order and rectitude.
>
> "The Roman emperors will also lose the royal dignity by which they before governed the empire and will see their glory wane, so that, by the permission of God, their power will diminish and degenerate little by little in their hands because of their lukewarm, servile, vain, useless, and impure lives. They would fain still be respected and honored by the people; but, as they will not seek the happiness of their subjects, they will no longer be esteemed by them. For this reason, the princes and rulers of many countries will break off from the Roman empire to its great detriment. Each country will choose its own king and say that the immense extent of the Roman empire is rather a burden than an honor. Ambition and greediness will so dazzle the hearts of these new princes that they will refuse to act according to the truth which they had learned, and to learn the things of which they will be ignorant.

"When the imperial sceptre shall have become so divided, beyond the possibility of being reunited, the tiara of the apostolic dignity shall be rent also. Princes and others, ecclesiastics and laymen, finding no religion around them, will disdain its authority and choose other masters or archbishops under divers titles, in the various provinces, and the Pope will fall so greatly from the exalted dignity which he formerly held, that he will hardly be able to perserve under his tiara, Rome, and a small tract of the surrounding country.

"Now all these things will be brought about in part by wars and also by the consent of other states, ecclesiastical or lay, for all will vie with each other to enable each temporal prince to constitute and govern his kingdom by his own power. Then many will return to the rules and customs of former times. But a short time will then elapse before the coming of the Son of Perdition, who will elevate himself above all that is called God, and before God at last will destroy him by the spirit of his mouth."

She describes the coming of the Antichrist as a parody of the divine Incarnation.

"For Christ did not come either at the beginning or the end of time; he came towards the evening (ad vesperam) when the heat of the day was past. What, then, came to pass? He opened the marrow of the law and gave issue to the great streams of virtue. In his person, he gave holy virginity to the world, and the divine germs, fertilized by the Spirit, were able to throw out their roots in the hearts of men.

"But the homicide in his turn will come suddenly; he will come at the hour when the sun goes down and the night follows day. O faithful ones, harken to this testimony and keep it as a safeguard in your memory so that the Man of Sin, coming unawares, may not draw your attention into perdition. Gird on the armor of faith and prepare for a great combat.

"The Man of Sin will be born of an ungodly woman who, from her infancy, will have been initiated into occult sciences and the wiles of *the demon*. She will live in the desert with perverse men, and abandon herself to crime with so much the greater ardour, *as she will think she is authorized thereto by the revelations of an angel*. And thus, in the fire of burning concupiscence she will conceive the Son of Perdition, without knowing by what father. Then she will teach that fornication is permitted, declare herself holy and be honored as a saint.

"But Lucifer, the old and cunning serpent, will find the fruit of her womb with his infernal spirit and entirely possess the fruit of sin.

"Now when he shall have attained the age of manhood, he will set himself up as a new master and teach perverse doctrine. Soon he will revolt against the saints; and he will acquire such great power that in the madness of his pride he would raise himself above the clouds; and, as in the beginning Satan said: I will be like unto the Most High, and fell; so in the last days, he will fall when he will say in the person of his son: I am the Savior of the world!

"He will ally himself with the kings, the princes and the powerful ones of the earth; he will condemn humility and will extol all the doctrines of pride. His magic art will feign the most astounding prodigies; he will disturb the atmosphere, command thunder and tempest, produce hail and horrible lightning; he will move mountains, dry up streams, reanimate the withered verdure of forests. His arts will be practiced upon all the elements, but chiefly upon man will he exhaust his infernal power. He will seem to take away health and restore it; he will drive out devils and raise the dead. How so? By sending some possessed soul into a dead body, to move it for a time. But these resurrections will be of short duration.

"At sight of these things, many will be terrified and will believe in him; and some, preserving their primitive faith, will nevertheless court the favors of the Man of Sin or fear his displeasure. And so many will be led astray among those who, shutting the interior eye of their souls, will live habitually in exterior thing. . . ."*

When, at last, the Antichrist has ascended a high mountain and been destroyed by the Lord, Hildegarde says that "many erring souls will return to truth, and men will make rapid progress in the ways of holiness."

It was reported that on the evening of St. Hildegarde's death, in her 82nd year, an extraordinary phenomenon occurred. Across the sky above the convent of Rupertsberg appeared two brilliant rainbows. At the point in midheaven where they intersected, was a bright radiance in the center of which there appeared a flaming cross.

HOLZHAUSER, BARTHOLOME (1613–1658).   German priest, prophet, and founder of a religious order known as the United Brothers or Bartholomites. He

* Hildergarde, *Scivias*.

was the eldest of eleven children of a poor family living in Langna, Bavaria.

Like most visionaries, he was endowed with the prophetic spirit from early youth.

In his commentary on the *Apocalypse* of John, *Interpretatio Apocalypsis usque ad cap XV*, he restates the central theme which informed the earlier work of Joachim of Flori (q.v.), the seven ages of the Church.

The fifth age, which corresponds to the present epoch, he termed *purgativas* and predicted that it would be characterized by universal calamities and terrible wars. The faithful would be persecuted and the Church stripped of its property.

After his death, a petition was started in Rome, seeking his canonization; but he was never made a saint.

HORBIGER, HANS (b. 1860).   An Austrian scientist, cosmogonist and radical theorist, he was born in Vienna on November 29, 1860. He made a fortune as the inventor and manufacturer of valves. This enabled him to retire at the age of 34 to devote himself to a study of cosmology.

He eventually propounded a theory of the origin of the cosmos which wholly rejected orthodox beliefs. He attacked empirical science as "a pernicious invention, a totem of decadence."

Horbiger maintained that only the inspired prophet, the illumined thinker, could arrive at truth.

His theory, which he called *Welt-Eis-Lehre* (Cosmic Ice Theory) was published in 1913. According to his system, there is an eternal conflict between ice and fire. All space, he said, is permeated by rarefied gases. The stars and planets are swimming in this gaseous or Cosmic Cloud. When the gases of hydrogen and oxygen come together in correct proportion, they combine to form water, which freezes instantly. This ice, in turn, is the beginning of solid matter.

Horbiger asserts that our solar system was formed when a colossal sun, a hundred times as large and bright as our own, collided with an enormous planet composed of cosmic ice. The planets of our solar system were the result of that collision; the ice planet penetrated deeply into the giant sun, and the huge explosion which followed threw out into space fragments of various sizes. These became the moon, Jupiter, Saturn, Mars, and so on.

Louis Pauwels and Jacques Bergier, in their work, *The Morning of the Magicians*, wrote that Horbiger's system not only postulates a history of our solar system and the birth of life and spirit on earth, but that it "describes the entire past of the universe and tells what its future transformations will be like.

Horbiger was a supporter of Adolph Hitler. The Nazi dictator found in the Austrian's theories confirmation of his own speculations concerning the world and the new superman.

HUBBARD, L. RON (b. 1911).

Founder of the Church of Scientology and originator of Dianetics, the modern science of mental health; philosopher, explorer, writer. He was born in Tilden, Nebraska, on March 13, 1911. His father was Comdr. Harry Ross Hubbard of the U.S. Navy, and his mother Dora May Hubbard (née Waterbury de Wolfe.)

Hubbard's early years were spent on a large cattle ranch in Montana, where long days were spent riding, breaking broncos, hunting coyote and taking his first steps as an explorer.

He was a precocious and diligent student, and his mother—a highly educated woman—encouraged his natural thirst for knowledge, supplementing his public schooling with private instruction at home. By the time he was 10 years old, he had already read a large number of the world's classics. He had also begun to develop an interest in philosophy and religion.

While pursuing these academic interests, Hubbard also found time to indulge his taste for travel and adventure. While he was still in his teens, his father was posted to the Far East, providing the youth with an opportunity to explore out-of-the-way places and to observe many exotic peoples and customs. He said later that it was during this period in Northern China and India, that his friendship and study with the holy men and teachers of Asia quickened his already keen interest in the subject of man's mental faculties and spiritual destiny.

Upon the death of his grandfather when Ron was 18, the Hubbard family returned to the United States and, after a course of preparatory study at Swavely School in Manassas, Virginia, and at Woodward Preparatory School in Washington, D.C., he enrolled in the George Washington University engineering school. Here he attended one of the first courses in nuclear physics to be taught in an American university.

During his college career, the wide range of Hubbard's mind became evident. His extra curricular activities included learning to fly and to become a skilled glider pilot; edit the college newspaper; take up photography; and support himself by writing technical articles for aviation and sports magazine.

While still a student, he directed the Caribbean Motion Picture Expedition. Later, in 1940, he was elected a member of the prestigious Explorers Club of New York and awarded the club flag for conducting the Alaskan Radio Experimental Expedition. Carrying the club flag on an expedition is considered a signal honor not easily won.

At the outbreak of World War II, Hubbard was ordered to the Philippines. He survived the early war in the Pacific, but was later severely wounded and in 1944 was hospitalized in the Oak Knoll Naval Hospital, crippled and blinded. He spent nearly a year at Oak Knoll, during which time he synthesized what he had learned of Eastern philosophy, his understanding of nuclear physics, and his life experience. "I set out to find from nuclear physics and a knowledge of the physical universe things entirely lacking in the Asian philosophy," he declared. It was during this period that some of the basic principles of Dianetics and Scientology were first formulated.

By 1947, he had fully recovered from his war wounds —partly, he claimed, as the result of applying mental techniques he had learned from an officer of the Naval Medical Corps, a Comdr. Thompson, who had been a personal pupil of Sigmund Freud.

In 1949, Hubbard wrote *Dianetics, The Original Thesis*, his first formal report of his discoveries concerning the mind and life. The manuscript was extensively copied and passed quickly from hand to hand among students of many countries.

What was needed, Hubbard reasoned, was a popular text on the subject which would answer the many questions contained in the letters which began to pour in, asking for clarification and advice. A publisher, Hermitage House, was eager to print such a book, but imposed one condition: the manuscript would have to be delivered in six weeks.

Hubbard complied and in six weeks had the completed book ready for publication. He characterized his work as "the anatomy of the mind." It included a technique called auditing—a process defined as command procedure which gets rid of unwanted mental barriers that inhibit, stop, or blunt a person's natural abilities, as well as gradiently increasing the abilities the person already possesses, so that he becomes more able, and his survival, happiness and intelligence increase enormously. He entitled the work, *Dianetics: The Modern Science of Mental Health.*

With publication of the text in 1950, Hubbard sprang suddenly to world-wide recognition. It quickly topped the *New York Times* best-seller list, where it remained for a considerable time.

Amid the flurry of lectures, news interviews, and organizational duties in setting up a Dianetics foundation following the success of his work, Hubbard continued his researches.

His further investigations brought to light even higher levels of processing than those developed by Dianetics. The expanded system he called Scientology, a word derived from the Latin *scio*, meaning "to know"; and the Greek "logos" or word, meaning the outward form by which the inward thought is expressed.

Thus the new and still advancing system became an applied religious philosophy. It now reached beyond the limited aims of self-improvement and into the vast spiritual realms, where such matters as the nature and function of the soul, the problems of time and eternity, the question of salvation; and learning how to "be at cause" knowingly and at will over thought, life, form, matter, energy, space and time, subjective and objective, must be dealt with.

Roy Wallis, an English scholar whose doctoral thesis at Oxford University was a study of Scientology, characterized the transformation as one which elevated Hubbard from the status of what he called (albeit incorrectly) a mystagogue to that of exemplary prophet.

"Hubbard had located a means of transcending human limitation and the downward spiral of man's spiritual nature. Like Buddha, he had made available a route to Total Freedom."*

Hubbard has been deeply concerned with the future of mankind, and has expressed the view that looking ahead is an essential dynamic of sane behavior. "There is a basic rule," he wrote in *Scientology: A New Slant on Life*, "that a psychotic person is concerned with the past; a neurotic person is barely able to keep up with the present; and a sane person is concerned with the future."

An unrelenting foe of radical psychiatric treatments which harm mental patients, Hubbard has predicted the imminent collapse of both psychiatry and psychoanalysis, as those disciplines are practiced today.

Hubbard foresees a rise in the religious consciousness of the world, largely through the efforts of young people such as those who comprise his church's Volunteer Ministers corps. At the same time, he warns of the danger to society of loss of faith:

"No culture in the history of the world, save the thoroughly depraved and expiring ones, has failed to affirm the existence of a Supreme Being. It is an empirical observation that men without a strong and lasting faith in a Supreme Being are less capable, less ethical, and less valuable to themselves and to society. A government wishing to deprave its people to the point where they will accept the most perfidious and rotten acts, abolishes first the concept of God; and in the wake of that, destroys the famliy with free love; the intellectual with police-enforced idiocies; and so reduces a whole population to an estate somewhat below that of dogs."

* Roy Wallis, *The Road to Total Freedom*. London, 1976.

As long ago as 1951, Hubbard forecast the rise of the Women's Movement and accurately described the dangers that would be inherent in it

"A race which . . . believes that the contest of the sexes in the spheres of business and politics is a worthier endeavor than the creation of tomorrow's generation, is a race which is dying. We have in the woman who is an ambitious rival of the man in his own activities, a woman who is neglecting the most important mission she may have. A society which looks down upon this mission and in which women are taught *anything but* the management of a family, the care of men, and the creation of the future generation, is a society which is on its way out.

"The historian can peg the point where a society begins its sharpest decline at the instant when women begin to take part, on an equal footing with men, in political and business affairs; since this means that the men are decadent and the women are no longer women. This is not a sermon on the role or position of women; it is a statement of bald and basic fact. When children become unimportant to a society, that society has forfeited its future. Even beyond the fathering and bearing and rearing of children, a human being does not seem to be complete without a relationship with the opposite sex. This relationship is the vessel wherein is nurtured the life force of both individuals, whereby they create the future of the race in body and thought.

"If man is to rise to greater heights, then woman must rise with him, or even before him. But she must rise *as* woman and not as today she is being misled into rising—as a man. It is the hideous joke of frustrated, unvirile men to make women over into the travesty of men which men themselves have become.

"Men are difficult and troublesome creatures—but valuable. The creative care and handling of men is an artful and beautiful task. Those who would cheat women of their rightful place by making them into men should at least realize that by this action they are destroying not only the women, but the men and children as well. This is too great a price to pay for being 'modern' or for someone's petty anger or spite against the female sex.

"The arts and skills of woman, the creation and inspiration of which she is capable and which, here and there in isolated places in our culture, she still manages to effect, in spite of the ruin and decay of man's world which spreads around her, must be brought newly and fully into life. These arts and skills and creation and inspiration are her beauty, just as she is the beauty of mankind."

The Church of Scientology today claims several million followers throughout the world, many of whom retain their membership in other churches at the same time.

ISRAEL IN PROPHECY. Prophecy has rightfully been called the heartthrob of the lawful religion of Israel. The sensitive ear of the divinely gifted Hebrew prophet could hear the voice of God and thereafter deliver His message to the people. That message could be one of exhortation, comfort or warning.

Most of the Old Testament prophets denounced in thunderous tones what they saw as a widespread depravity in the society of their day. They tried to their utmost to instill in their wayward contemporaries a deep fear of God's retribution. In particular, they inveighed against idolatry, a sin to which the Scripture clearly shows the Jews were inclined, partly as a result of their sojourn in Egypt and partly from the influence of their heathen neighbors.

It is quite remarkable (and significant) that while the Jewish prophets came mostly from the lower ranks of life and had but limited formal education, they were able not only to make brilliant assessments of their own nation, isolated by natural boundaries and religious restrictions, but of other countries they had never seen.

In its amazing scope, their prophetic reach extended from the fall of man, across millenia of human history, to the consummation of all things.

One of the great themes of all Hebrew prophecy was the future advent of a Messiah, "the annointed one," destined to deliver Israel from the power of its foreign oppressors.

Many evangelical Christian sects believe that Israel plays a divinely ordained role in world history and that future events can be forecast on the basis of what is happening in the ancient Jewish homeland. "If you want to know where we are in history, look at the Jewish people," declared a full-page newspaper announcement sponsored by a hundred Christian churches. "They are God's timepiece and people of prophecy. Part of an eternal clock ticking away. . ."

Millenarians mark the beginning of the pre-apocalyptic period with the rebirth of Israel as a nation. The second "sign of the times" was the unification of Jerusalem under Jewish rule. The third, and final, important event, which will usher in the period of wars and tribulation that will precede the second Advent, will be the building of the Third Temple.

According to these interpreters of biblical prophecy, the rebuilding of the Temple will be followed by an invasion of foreign armies which will besiege Jerusalem. The Temple's holy of holies will be desecrated. But the enemy will be defeated and, with the triumphant second advent of Jesus Christ, the long-awaited millenium of peace will begin.

Another and quite different prediction concerning the destiny of Israel is contained in the Prophecy of Premol (q. v.), dating from about the seventeenth century. Its author is unknown; the manuscript was found among some ancient documents belonging to the former administrator of the monastery of Premol in Grenoble, France:

"With a roll of thunder, the clouds parted and I beheld Jerusalem laid low by a frightful tempest; its walls had fallen as from the blows of a battering ram, and blood ran through the streets; the enemy had taken possession of the city.

"The abomination of desolation ruled the city.

"And is was here that I beheld the Patriarch emerge from the Temple that had been invaded by the sons of Baal. He fled, carrying with him the Ark of the Covenant, and fled toward the sea where the sun sets."

After witnessing the annihilation of Israel, the unknown prophet concludes: "Afterward, I beheld upon the horizon a brilliant conflagration. Then my vision clouded over and I neither saw nor heard anything more. Then the Spirit said to me: 'This is the beginning of the last days of earth.' And I awoke terrified."

JOACHIM OF FLORIS (1145–1202). A famous visionary hermit, Cistercian monk and church reformer, he
was born in Celico, Calabria, Italy, in A.D. 1145.

During his youth, he made a number of pilgrimages
to holy places. Following one of these, during which he
spent a period of time in an ascetic retreat, he became
a monk in the Cistercian abbey of Casamari. Later,
however, he left the Cistercian order to found a rule of
his own, with an abbey at San Giovanni di Fiore.

Joachim was a prolific writer of prophecy and theology. Among the most widely circulated of his works
were commentaries on the Old Testament prophets—
Jeremiah, Isaiah and Ezekiel; an exegesis on the Apocalypse of John; a treatise on the prophecies of the Eri-
trean Sybil; and his celebrated work, *Prophecy of the
Eternal Gospel*.

Joachim divides human history into three ages, which
he designated by names corresponding to the Holy
Trinity—that is, the ages of the Father, the Son, and

the Holy Spirit. The reign of the Father was the time of the Old Testament, of the Law; that of the Son was the age of the New Testament, of faith, and of grace; it ended in 1260 A.D., at which time the third and final age of man, that of the Holy Spirit, began.

The last age, according to Joachim, began in the year 1260 with the establishment of the monks in the West, and will last until the end of the world.

During this final period of the Holy Spirit, a complete transformation of man's religious life will occur. Joachim predicted the end of the papacy, to be succeeded by a new kind of church rooted in a spiritual interpretation of the Gospels.

> "Peter [that is, the Pope] will disappear, giving way to John [the Revealer], because the reign of the Holy Spirit will be the reign of the free.
> "In the first age of the world, there were slaves; in the second, free men; in the third, communities of friends. In the first, law dominated; in the second, grace; and in the third there will be a fuller and more liberal grace. In the first age—servile bondage, chastisement, domination of the old, winter. In the second—wisdom, progeny, the light of morning, spring, shoots of the corn and vine, children. In the third—the beginning of real freedom, contemplation, charity, friends, shade, summer, corn, oil, and the Easter of resurrection."

Joachim saw evil invading the Church, which he called "a den of thieves;" and he prophesied God's wrath against it. The clergy, he said, were loathed because of their baseness and corruption; the prelates were avaricious plunderers; and the Antichrist would occupy the papal throne itself.

"Rome, a city devoid of all Christian discipline, is

the fountain-head of all the abominations in Christendom, and upon her will fall the first judgment of God."

Strangely enough, Joachim was not censured by the three popes through whose pontificates he lived, despite his denunciation of the hierarchy and his prophecy that the papacy would end. It was not until ten years after his death that his prophecies were officially condemned by the Lateran Council of 1212, under Pope Innocent III. In 1216, another council held at Arles condemned all Joachim's works and his followers as well.

His work was widely acclaimed throughout Italy and France, where it found favor especially with the anti-papal movement of the time, a movement that was to culminate in the Reformation, which rejected the Vatican's supremacy once and for all.

The Joachimites organized formal study courses and lectures to acquire a deeper knowledge of the seer's work. In his *Divine Comedy*, Dante, an avowed admirer of Joachim, placed the mystic abbot in Paradise, while at the same time assigning the Pope a place in the circle of Hell.

KANAKUK (d. 1852).   Prophet of the Kickapoo tribe of
American Indians. He exhorted his people to remain in
their Illinois homeland when the federal government
assigned the tribe a reservation in Missouri, where
they were opposed by hostile Osages, already settled
there.

   Kanakuk prophesied that the Kickapoos would in-
herit a land of natural abundance, if they would eschew
alcohol, put a stop to their intra-tribal squabbles, and
daily supplicate the Great Spirit, using special prayer
sticks carved with sacred symbols.

   Eventually, the tribe was settled in Kansas.

KOLASKIN (19th century).   Prophet, shaman and chief
of the Sanpoil tribe of American Indians in the State of
Washington.

   There are many stories and legends about Kolaskin,
but few authenticated facts. He led an unremarkable

life until his mid-twenties, when he was stricken with a mysterious illness which caused his body to swell and become covered with boils. His legs were completely paralyzed.

After suffering two years from this malady, Kolaskin apparently died. As his family and friends prepared him for burial, he suddenly came to life and began to sing a strange song no one had ever heard before.

Kolaskin told his astonished friends that while in the death state, the Great Spirit had told him to return to life and to preach a new doctrine to the Indians, one which adjured them to lead a moral life, renouncing all liquor, adultery and theft. They were instructed to say special prayers each morning and evening, before meals, and on the eve of a hunt or any undertaking of importance.

Kolaskin announced that it had been revealed to him during a trance that a devastating flood was about to overwhelm the earth, and that his followers could only save themselves by building an ark, as Noah did in ancient times.

The ark-building went forward at a rapid pace until the federal government intervened and halted the activity.

While the flood did not come as Kolaskin had predicted, several earthquakes that he had foretold did occur at the time he designated, and his cult continued to grow.

The U.S. government eventually arrested and imprisoned Kolaskin in a federal penitentiary, charging that he had established a tyrannical rule over his followers and caused constant fighting among members of his tribe.

When he was released, he no longer prophesied publicly. After his death, his cult continued into the 1930s.

LAKE, HANDSOME (1735–1815).   An Iroquois prophet and founder of the Good Message cult, he was born
in 1735 near Avon, New York. He was a member of
the Wolf clan of the Seneca tribe. He was reared and
educated by a group of Quakers, whose beliefs and
practices helped shape his later teachings.

Handsome Lake (his Indian name was Ganioda'yo)
founded his prophetic mystique in 1799. The new religion required its adherents to abstain from alcohol in
any form; to reject witchcraft and shamanistic rituals;
and to practice a form of meditation aimed at allowing
the light of the Great Spirit to illuminate the individual's soul.

Handsome Lake experienced his first prophetic vision
on June 15, 1799, as he lay in a coma, apparently dying
of an incurable disease. He heard a voice which told
him to arise and go into the surrounding forest. As
weak as he was, he summoned up enough strength to
do as the voice instructed.

Outside, Handsome Lake encountered three phantom messengers of the Great Spirit, who cured his terminal illness by having him eat the fruit from three branches they gave him. His spirit guides then showed him an Indian version of heaven and hell, the latter inhabited by evil spirits busy loading barrels of whiskey on their canoes.

In a later vision, Handsome Lake beheld the Great Spirit himself, who once more cautioned him concerning the evils of intemperance, and bade him go forth to preach a new faith, which would proscribe the use of firewater, strengthen the bonds of families, and to rear Indian children in the traditions of their tribe. Intermarriage with whites was forbidden because the Great Spirit had created the Iroquois as a distinct people and wished them to retain their identity.

After the prophet's death in 1815, he was succeeded by his nephew Soseha'wa as leader of the cult.

LE ROYER, JEANNE (1732–1798).   A lay sister in a convent at Fougêres, near the city of Rennes, in Brittany.

In a series of visions, in which she said Jesus Christ appeared to her, she foresaw the calamities which years later were to desolate France.

Like other ecstatics, she prophesied wars, earthquakes and social upheavals to occur before the appearance of the Antichrist.

Weighing the information she had gleaned from her visions, the seeress predicted the time of the end would come about the year 2000, following the end of the papacy.

Although Sister Nativité (as she was known) was taught to read, she was unable to write. She dictated her revelations to her director, the Abbé Genét, who later published them.

MALACHY, ST. (1094–1148), known also as Maedoc Va Morgair. Irish archbishop and seer, was born in Armagh, Ireland, in 1094. He is said to have been of noble lineage on his father's side.

In the Ireland of St. Malachy's day, even more than now, the gift of prophecy or of clairvoyance was not unusual. There was hardly a clan that did not possess at least one visionary, who could foretell future events.

It is not extraordinary, then, that an 11th-century Irish monk who from his youth had been steeped in the mysticism of Celtic religious traditions should show early signs of having psychic talent.

What *is* extraordinary, however, is the fact that his most celebrated prophecy covers a period of almost a thousand years, or from 1143 until the end of time, estimated to occur around the year 2000.

St. Bernard, Malachy's good friend and biographer, tells how his contemporaries learned of his ability to foretell future events. He says that the Irish abbot, who was staying at a monastery in Clonmel, told his fellow monks that a certain youth whom he indicated in a crowd would ask his help in being received into their order. As he predicted, the following day, the youth did come to Malachy. "From this, the brethren knew that Malachy had the spirit of prophecy."

In 1139, Malachy left Ireland to make what in those days was an arduous journey to Rome for the purpose of asking the Pope for the pallium (a special church vestment) for the Archbishop of Armagh, as a sign that he shared in the supreme pastoral power.

En route to the Holy See, Malachy visited the Cistercian monastery at Clairvaux, France, where he met St. Bernard, who was abbot and founder of the convent. The two formed a deep and lasting friendship.

According to an account written by the Abbé Cucherat, it was during his stay in Rome that Malachy beheld in a vision the long succession of 112 pontiffs who were to follow Celestinus II (1143), before the final fall of Rome when "the awful Judge will judge the people."

Malachy wrote down his revelation, accompanying the name of each future pope with a device or motto related to his family name or background; or some circumstance of his life. The meaning of these Latin appelations would become known in the course of time.

Cucherat writes that the manuscript of Malachy's strange prophecy was presented to Pope Innocent II, who eventually assigned it to the Vatican archives, where it remained forgotten for four hundred years.

As a matter of factual history, the famous composition was first made public in 1595 by a Benedictine historian named Arnold Wion. He included it casually in his work, *Lignum Vitae*, published in Venice, with these words of explanation:

"Malachy is said to have written some treatises, none of which I have come across except a prophecy concerning the sovereign pontiffs. As it is short and, so far as I know, has never been printed, and because many desire to see it, I insert it here."

Because of the long delay in its publication, and the fact that the devices of the pontiffs down to the year 1590 appear to fit more accurately than later ones, the authorship of the celebrated prophecy has been challenged by a number of critics, notably the two Jesuits, Claudio Francisco Menestrier and Juan Planella, and the German theologian, Bellesheim.

Most of the arguments put forward to disprove the authenticity of the prophecy have been ably refuted by scholars who believed in its validity and authorship. The definitive work in the latter field was that of Joseph Maître, abbot of Baume, published in Paris in 1902. In 1972, the Spanish writer, Jose Corral published a work, *El fin del mundo esta muy cerca* in which he refutes the principal impeachments of the Malachy prophecies.

In the final analysis, the authorship of the prophetic document is not so important as the question of its accuracy. Of the 112 popes in the long series, only four remain after Paul VI until the end of the world.

There has been much speculation regarding the devices of the future pontiffs, and attempts to determine something of their identities or character from the Latin phrases.

The successor to Paul VI is designated by the motto: *De medietate lunae* (from the center of the moon). Several commentators have suggested that the translation of the Latin words should be "from a half moon" and interpret it to mean an antipope, since the moon has been used in the past as a symbol for the Church. Such a reading presupposes a schism and in that respect at least may be well founded, since the rebellion against the papal rule of Paul VI, launched by Archbishop Marcel Lefebvre of France, is spreading throughout the world.

Another interpretation is that the device may refer to the Islamic world and presage an attack on the Vatican by forces of an Arab alliance, as prophesied by Nostradamus. E. M. Ruir, a commentator on Nostradamus, writes that an antipope is foreshadowed, the beast that "will talk like the Lamb and will imitate him." The true Pope will be taken captive and deported into an Arab country, where he will end his life.

Jose Corral also interprets *De medietate lunae* to mean an antipope, who will act as a false prophet for the coming Antichrist predicted in the Apocalypse of St. John, 13:11–12. He surmises that the symbol of the moon in the device may refer to the city of Sarzana, Italy, as it did in the case of Pope Nicholas V (1447), who came from that town and to whom St. Malachy assinged the appelation *De modicitate lunae*. (The ancient name for the city was Luna.)

Or, adds Corral, the moon symbol may refer to a detail of the future pope's family arms.

The pope immediately following *De medietate lunae* on St. Malachy's list carries a device related to the sun, namely, *De labore solis* (From the sun's labor). Some scholars say the phrase could be translated, "From the work, or the result of the sun's labor."

The only previous reference to the sun in the roll of 122 popes, was that in the designation of Alexander V (1409), an antipope: *Flagellum solis* (the scourge of the sun). This fact has provided the rather unconvincing conclusion by several interpreters that this pontiff will also be an antipope. It has been suggested that he and his predecessor, the "lunar" pope, will usher in the time of great tribulations, which the prophet Joel foresaw:

"And I will show wonders in the heavens and in the earth, blood and fire and pillars of smoke. The sun shall be turned into darkness, and the moon into blood, before the great and terrible day of the Lord come." (Joel 2:30–31)

The device signalling the penultimate pope, according to St. Malachy, will be: *De gloria olivae* (from the glory of the olive). Aside from its familiar use to symbolize peace, the olive branch is also an emblem of the Jewish people. In both the Old and New Testaments, there are repated references to them which employ that symbol.

In consequence, a number of commentators have surmised that the olive symbol in the present instance presages a period of peace during which the prophesied conversion of the Jews will occur. They cite the letter of Paul to the Romans, in which he writes:

"But I have something to say to you Gentiles. I am a missionary to the Gentiles, and as such I give all honour to that ministry when I try to stir emulation in the men of my own race, and so to save some of them. For if their rejection has meant the reconciliation of the world, what will their acceptance mean? Nothing less than life from the dead! If the first portion of dough is consecrated, so is the whole lump. If the root is consecrated, so are the branches. But if some of the branches have been lopped off, and you, a wild olive, have been grafted in among them, and have come to share the same root and sap as the olive, do not make yourself superior to the branches. If you do so, remember that it is not you who sustain the root: the root sustains you.

"You will say, 'Branches were lopped off so that I

might be grafted in.' Very well: they were lopped off for lack of faith, and by faith you hold your place. Put away your pride, and be on your guard; for if God did not spare the native branches, no more will he spare you. Observe the kindness and the severity of God—severity to those who fell away, divine kindness to you, if only you remain within its scope; otherwise you too will be cut off, whereas they, if they do not continue faithless, will be grafted in; for it is in God's power to graft them in again. For if you were cut from your native wild olive and against all nature grafted into the cultivated olive, how much more readily will they, the natural olive-branches, be grafted into their native stock!

"For there is a deep truth here, my brothers, of which I want you to take account, so that you may not be complacent about your own discernment: this partial blindness has come upon Israel only until the Gentiles have been admitted in full strength; when that has happened, the whole of Israel will be saved, in agreement with the text of Scripture:

" 'From Zion shall come the Deliverer; / He shall remove wickedness from Jacob. / And this is the covenant I will grant them, / When I take away their sins.' " (Romans : 13–27).

The final ecclesiarch to occupy the chair of Peter, according to Malachy's prophecy, will be known simply as Peter of Rome (Petrus Romanus).

In his work on prophecy, entitled *After Nostradamus*, A. Woldben, expresses the view that the pontificate of the Roman Peter will see the general destruction of the Church, but that a remnant of faithful will survive. The appelation, he says, forecasts more than just the name of a person; it indicates a last epoch that will be in contrast to that of Peter the Apostle who initiated it.

The time of this pope will be that of the great tribulation which will end an age. He will be the Pope of the Apocalypse and will witness the ruin of everything and the destruction of everything before complete renewal. The final Antichrist will enter the scene.

> "But in the general destruction there will remain some who will see the new day, and life will be revived, renovated for a new cycle.
>
> "The end of the Papacy will have no connection with the vitality of religion and the faith which is in the heart of every man. Institutions can change just as exterior manifestations of religion can take different forms. What cannot alter is the substance and no material force can ever touch it."

St. Malachy himself adds a final word to his prophecy, a terminal postscript that admits of no such gloss as that just quoted. His concluding prediction reads:

> "During the last persecution of the Holy Roman Church, there shall sit Peter of Rome, who shall feed the sheep amid great tribulations, and when these have passed, the City of the Seven Hills shall be utterly destroyed, and the awful Judge will judge the people."

Following are a full list of the papal mottos listed by St. Malachy:

EX CASTRO TIBERIS (From the castle on the Tiber)—Celestine II (1143–1144).
INIMICUS EXPULSUS (The enemy driven out)—Lucius II (1144–1145).

EX MAGNITUDINE MONTIS (From the greatness of a mountain)—Eugene III (1145–1153).

ABBAS SUBURRANUS (A Suburran abbot)—Anastasius IV (1153–1154).

DE RURE ALBO (From a white country place)—Adrian IV (1154–1159).

EX ANSERE CUSTODI (From the keeper goose)—Alexander III (1159–1181).

DE TETRO CARCERE (From a foul prison)—Victor IV, Antipope (1159–1164).

VIA TRANSTIBERNIA (The way beyond the Tiber)—Paschal III, Antipope (1164–1168).

DE PANNOMIA TUSCIAE (From the Hungary of Tuscia)—Calixtus III, Antipope (1168–1178).

LUX IN OSTIO (A light in the gate)—Lucius III (1181–1185).

SUS IN CRIBRO (A sow in a sieve)—Urban III (1185–1187).

ENSIS LAURENTII (The sword of Lawrence)—Gregory VIII (1187).

DE SCHOLA EXIET (He will come out of a school)—Clement III (1187–1191).

DE RURE BOVENSI (From the cattle country)—Celestine III (1191–1198).

COMES SIGNATUS (A signed count)—Innocent III (1198–1216).

CANONICUS DE LATERE—(A Canon from the side)—(1216–1226).

AVIS OSTIENSIS (The bird of Ostia)—Gregory IX (1227–1241).

LEO SABINUS (The Sabine lion)—Celestine IV (1241).

COMES LAURENTIUS (Count Lawrence)—Innocent IV (1243–1254).

SIGNUM OSTIENSE (A sign of Ostia)—Alexander IV (1254–1261).

HIERUSALEM CAMPANIAE (Jerusalem of Champagne)—Urban IV (1261–1264).

DRACO DEPRESSUS (A crushed serpent)—Clement IV (1265–1268).

ANGUINEUS VIR (A snakelike man)—Gregory X (1271–1276).

CONCIONATUR GASSUS (A French preacher)—Innocent V (1276).

BONUS COMES (A good count)—Adrian V (1276).

PISCATOR TUSCUS (A Tuscian fisherman)—John XXI (1276–1277).

ROSA COMPOSITA (A compounded Rose)—Nicholas III (1277–1280).

EX TELONIO LILIACEI MARTINI (From the receipt of custom of Martin of the lilies)—Martin IV (1281–1285).

EX ROSA LEONINA (From a leonine rose)—Honorius IV (1285–1287).

PICUS INTER ESCAS (A woodpecker among the food) —Nicholas IV (1288–1292).

EX EREMO CELSUS (The lofty one from the desert)— Celestine V (1294).

EX UNDARUM BENEDICTIONE (From a blessing of the waves)—Boniface VIII (1294–1303).

CONCIONATOR PATAREUS (A preacher from Patara)—Benedict XI (1303–1304).

DE FOSSIS AQUITANICIS (From the ditches of Aquitaine)—Clement V (1205–1314).

DE SUTORE OSSEO (From a bony shoemaker)—John XXI or XXII (1316–1334).

CORVUS SCHISMATICUS (A schismatical crow)— Nicolas V, Antipope (1328–1338).

FRIGIDUS ABBAS (A cold abbot)—Benedict XII (1334–1342).

EX ROSA ATREBATENSI (From the rose of Arras— Clement VI (1342–1352).

DE MONTIBUS PAMMACHII (From the mountain of

Pammachius)—Innocent VI (1352–1362).

GALLUS VICECOMES (A French viscount)—Urban V (1362–1370).

NOVUS DE VIRGINE FORTI (A new man from a strong virgin)—Gregory XI (1370–1378).

DE INFERNO PREGNANI (The Pregnani from hell)—Urban VI (1378–1389).

DE CRUCE APOSTOLICA (From an apostolic cross)—Clement VII, Antipope (1378–1394).

CUBUS DE MIXTIONE (The square of mixture)—Boniface IX (1389–1404).

LUNA COSMEDIANA (The moon of Cosmedin)—Benedict XIII, Antipope (1394–1424).

DE MELIORE SIDERE (From a better star)—Innocent VII (1404–1406).

NAUTA DE PONTE NIGRO (A sailor from a black bridge)—Gregory XII (1406–1415).

FLAGELLUM SOLIS (The scourge of the sun)—Alexander V, Antipope (1409–1410).

CERVUS SYRENAE (The stag of the Syren)—John XXIII, Antipope (1410–1419).

COLUMNA VELI AURI (The pillar with the golden veil)—Martin V (1417–1431).

SCHISMA BARCHINONIUM (A schism of Barcelona)—Clement VIII, Antipope (1424–1429).

LUPA CAELESTINA (A Coelestinian she-wolf)—Eugene IV (1431–1437).

AMATOR CRUCIS (A lover of the cross)—Amadeus VIII (1439–1449).

DE MODICITATE LUNAE (From the littleness of the moon)—Nicolas V (1447–1455).

BOS PASCENS (A bull browsing)—Callistus III (1455–1458).

DE CAPRA ET ALBERGO (From a she-goat and a tavern)—Pius II (1458–1464).

DE CERVO ET LEONE (From a stag and a lion)—Paul II (1464–1471).

PISCATOR MINORITA (A Minorite fisherman)—Sixtus
   IV (1471–1481).

PRAECURSOR SICILIAE (A forerunner from Sicily)—
   Innocent VII (1484–1492).

BOS ALBANUS IN PORTU (An Alban bull in the Port)
   —Alexander VI (1492–1503).

DE PARVO HOMINE (From a little man)—Pius III
   (1503).

FRUCTUS JOVIS JUVABIT (The fruit of Jupiter will
   help)—Julius II (1503–1513).

DE CRATICULA POLITIANA (From a Politian grid-
   iron)—Leo X (1513–1521).

LEO FLORENTINUS (A lion of Florence)—Adrian VI
   (1522–1523).

FLOS PILAE (The flower of the ball)—Clement VIII (1523–
   1534).

HYACINTHUS MEDICUS (The jacinth physician)—
   Paul III (1534–1549).

DE CORONA MONTANA (Of the mountain crown)—
   Julius III (1550–1555).

FRUMENTUM FLOCCIDUM (Hairy grain)—Marcellus
   II (1555).

DE FIDE PETRI (Of the faith of Peter)—Paul IV (1555–
   1559).

AESCULAPII PHARMACUM (The drug of Aescula-
   pius)—Pius IV (1559–1567).

ANGELUS NEMOROSUS (A woodland angel)—Pius
   V (1566–1572).

MEDIUM CORPUS PILARUM (A half body of the
   balls)—Gregory XIII (1572–1585).

AXIS IN MEDIETATE SIGNI (An axis in the midst of
   a sign)—Sixtus V (1585–1590).

EX ANTIQUITATE URBIS (From the oldness of a city)
   —Gregory XIV (1590–1591).

PIA CIVITAS IN BELLO (A dutiful state in war)—
   Innocent IX (1591).

CRUX ROMULEA (A Roman cross)—Clement VIII (1592–1605).

UNDOSUS VIR (A wavy man)—Leo XI (1605).

GENS PERVERSA (A crooked people)—Paul V (1605–1621).

IN TRIBULATIONE PACIS (In tribulation of peace) —Gregory XV (1621–1623).

LILIUM ET ROSA (The lily and the rose)—Urban VIII (1623–1641).

JUCUNDITAS CRUCIS (The joy of the cross)—Innocent X (1644–1655).

MONTIUM CUSTOS (A keeper of mountains)—Alexander VII (1655–1667).

SYDUS OLORUM (A constellation of swans)—Clement IX (1667–1669).

DE FLUMINE MAGNO (From a great river)—Clement X (1670–1676).

BELLUA INSATIABILIS (An insatiable beast)—Innocent XI (1676–1680).

POENITENTIA GLORIOSA (Glorious penance)—Alexander VIII (1689–1691).

RASTRUM IN PORTA (The rake at the door)—Innocent XII (1691–1700).

FLORES CIRCUMDATI (Flowers set round about)—Clement XI (1700–1721).

DE BONA RELIGIONE (From a good religious order) —Innocent XIII (1721–1724).

MILES IN BELLO (A soldier in war)—Benedict XIII (1724–1730).

COLUMNA EXCELSA (A lofty pillar)—Clement XII (1730–1740).

ANIMAL RURALE (A country beast)—Benedict XIV (1740–1758).

ROSA UMBRIAE (A rose of Umbria)—Clement XIII (1758–1769).

URSUS VELOX (A swift bear)—Clement XIV (1769–1775).

PEREGRINUS APOSTOLICUS (An apostolic wanderer)—Pius VI (1775–1799).

AQUILA RAPAX (An eagle carrying away)—Pius VII (1800–1823).

CANIS ET COLUBER (A dog and an adder)—Leo XII (1823–1829).

VIR RELIGIOSUS (A religious man)—Pius VIII (1829–1831).

DE BALNEIS ETRURIAE (From the hot baths of Tuscany)—Gregory XVI (1832–1846).

CRUX DE CRUCE (The cross from a cross)—Pius IX (1846–1878).

LUMEN IN COELO (A light in the sky)—Leo XIII (1878–1903).

IGNIS ARDENS (Burning fire)—Pius X (1903–1914).

RELIGIO DEPOPULATA (Religion laid waste)—Benedict XV (1914–1922).

FIDES INTREPIDA (Faith undaunted)—Pius XI (1922–1939).

PASTOR ANGELICUS (An angelic shepherd)—Pius XII (1939–1958).

PASTOR ET NAUTA (A shepherd and a sailor)—John XXIII (1958–1963).

FLOS FLORUM (A flower of flowers)—Paul VI (1963–). *[John Paul I]*

DE MEDIETATE LUNAE (From a half-moon)— *John Paul I*

DE LABORE SOLIS (From the toil of the sun)— *John Paul II*

DE GLORIA OLIVAE (From the glory of the olive)—

PETRUS ROMANUS (Peter of Rome) —

MERLIN (A.D. 5th century).   The most famous of all British prophets is known to us only through many remarkable legends. Scholarly opinion is divided on the question of whether he was a real historical personage or a mythical folk hero.

J. J. Dollinger notes that he became the hero of a whole cycle of lengendary tales that became deeply rooted in medieval literature, not as a bard "in which character he is nowhere at all mentioned, but as a prophet, an enchanter, and the son of a demon."

The latter statement refers to a long-prevalent belief that Merlin was an offspring of Satan, who had had intercourse with a nun. In the Arthurian romance he was counsellor to King Arthur and lived at his court.

In 1152, Geoffrey of Monmouth, creator of the Arthur legend, incorporated the *Prophecies of Merlin* as the seventh book of his work, *Historia Britonum*. The composition exerted a powerful influence on the popular mind, not only in Britain, but in France, Italy and Germany as well.

Among the predictions attributed to Merlin are those foretelling the Crusades, the French Revolution, the eventual decline of Britain, the end of the papacy, the destruction of Rome, the final consummation of human history.

"There will be a pope who will not dare to so much as look upon Rome," declares one of his prophecies. "Similarly, one thing the Romans must understand, among others is that before the death of the pope, Our Lord will make him suffer such disgrace that there will be nothing to compare with it. It is likewise necessary that the Romans know, among other things, that from that time on will begin their destruction, step by step, and that it will be because of their sins."

In a curious work entitled *Sunday Prophecies of Merlin, Becket and Others*, published in London in 1652, the writer quotes another prophecy of Merlin regarding the future of England:

"Merlin saith that in England shall be seen many

strange things, as preaching of traytors, great rain and wind, great hunger among the common people, great oppression of blood, great imprisonment of many men and great battel; so that there shall be few or no quiet place to abide in; the Prince shall forsake men of the church, Lords shall foresake righteousness, counsel of aged men shall not be set by; religious men shall be thrust out of their houses; the common people for feare shall not know which way to turne them; parents shall be hated by their children, men of worship shall have no reverence of their inferiours; chastitie shall be broken with maidens, wives and widows, religious men and virgins, with more ill than I can tell of, from the which God us defend."

METHODIUS, ST. (d. circa 255).   Ecclesiastical author, prophet, bishop, suffered martyrdom during the persecution of Emperor Diocletian. He held the See Patara in Lycia, and later in Tyre.

His written works include treatises on free will, chastity, resurrection, and leprosy. Some scholars believe the prophecies attributed to him were by another author, who signed his name because of the bishop's great prestige and the fact that he had written a treatise on the Apocalypse. The manuscript was discovered several centuries after the death of Mothodius in the Patrum Veterum Library.

The revelations predict that Arab armies will spring forth from the deserts to subdue Christian lands. But an Emperor and his son will make a surprise attack upon the victorious invaders, just when they feel themselves most secure, and will drive them out of the conquered territories.

The coming of the Son of perdition is also foreseen:
"When the Son of Perdition appears, all principalities and powers will be overthrown. He will be of the

tribe of Dan, according to the prophecy of Jacob. This enemy of religion will use a diabolic art to produce many false miracles, such as causing the blind to see, the lame to walk and the deaf to hear. Those possessed with demons will be exorcised. He will deceive many and, if he could, as Our Lord has said, even the faithful elect.

"Even Antichrist will enter Jerusalem, where he will enthrone himself in the Temple as a god (even though he will be an ordinary man of the tribe of Dan to which Judas Iscariot also belonged.)

"In those days, the Antichrist will bring about many tribulations; but God will not allow those redeemed by the divine blood to be deceived. For that reason, he will send his two servants, Enoch and Elias, who will declare the prodigies of the Antichrist to be false, and will denounce him as a impostor. After the death and ruin of many, he will leave the Temple in confusion; and many of his followers will foresake him to join the company of the righteous. The seducer, upon seeing himself reproached and scorned, will become enraged and will put to death those saints of God. It is then that there will appear the sign of the Son of Man, and he will come upon the clouds of heaven."

MILLER, WILLIAM (1782–1849).   Founder and leader of the Adventist or Millerite movement in America, was born in Pittsfield, Massachusetts, immediately following the Revolutionary War.

He grew up on his family's 100-acre farm at Low Hampton, New York. Both Miller's parents were devout churchgoers, and their home was frequently the meeting place for services conducted by preachers passing through Low Hampton.

Although a formal education was denied him, young Miller was an avid student and omnivorous reader.

When he was fourteen, two prominent neighbors—one a judge, the other a Congressman—made their private libraries available to him.

In 1818, following two years' intensive study of the Scriptures, he reached the conclusion that the time of Christ's second advent was at hand:

> "Finding all the signs of the times and the present condition of the world, to compare harmoniously with the prophetic descriptions of the last days, I was compelled to believe that this world had about reached the limits of the period allotted for its continuance. As I regarded the evidence, I could arrive at no other conclusion."

In 1831, convinced that the world must be warned that the end was near, he began to give public lectures to expound his views. His new interpretation of Scripture, radical in those days, was firmly rejected by most of his contemporaries, who referred to him variously as "Crazy Miller, the end-o-the-worldman," "that fanatic" or "Miller the Prophet."

In his sermons, Miller argued that the passage in the Book of Daniel, 8:14, "unto 2300 days" was to be interpreted 2,300 years, beginning with the time the Prophet Ezra went up to Jerusalem in 457 B.C. The time indicated, therefore, would come to an end in 1843.

Miller was quiet and convincing in his expositions, speaking as he did from a positive conviction. Soon he had recruited a number of ministers and lay followers, who eagerly looked forward to the imminent fulfillment of prophecy, which would culminate with the second advent.

When the year 1843 passed without incident, Miller explained to his followers that he had erred in naming the year owing to having followed the Hebrew rather than the Roman chronology. Instead of 1843, the date of the second advent was definitely October 22, 1844.

In spite of the initial disappointment, his followers now accepted the new date with excitement and hope. In churches, halls, tabernacles and homes, meetings were held continuously during the two weeks preceding the announced date. In *The Prophetic Faith of Our Fathers*, Leroy Edwin Froom writes that:

"Intensity marked the closing days. A quickened tempo and greater urgency took possession of men, like the fervor of the crusaders of old, as the movement swept toward its intense but orderly climax. Their Boston steam presses rolled at top speed twenty-four hours a day, to turn out Adventist papers for distribution 'without money and without price,' and a dozen other presses ran day and night to supply the need. All the way from Maine out to Ohio, and from Canada down into the South, living messengers went from house to house in city and village, and from farm to farm in the country, with the last warning message."

Some Millerites, dressed in white robes, left their shops, homes and farms to await the coming of Christ on rooftops and hills. Froom has given a moving description of the event:

"At last, October 22 dawned, bright and clear. The Adventists repaired to their meetinghouses or held small religious services in their homes. They met at an early hour and continued in watchful prayer, meditation, and song most of the day. Those were solemn hours, hours big with hope—the last hours of time, they believed. They were standing on the brink of eternity, and would soon see Him whom, not having seen, they loved. They were at peace with all men, with every sin confessed. Their work was done, and they were anxiously awaiting the fulfillment of God's promise.

Within a few hours they believed the heavens would roll together as a scroll, the elements melt with fervent heat, and their Savior would appear. "From one home, as the day was ending and the Savior had not come, the sun was seen sinking over the western hills. Its last rays lighted up a cloud near the horizon, and it shone like burnished silver and gold. It was a glorious scene, and the father rose expectantly from his chair, thinking it might be the Savior coming. But it was only a 'sun-kissed cloud,' and the family resumed its waiting. Thus the day wore slowly on to its weary close, though far into the night the faithful kept vigil. But from those exalted heights they were soon dashed to the depths of despair. Their Lord came not, and the day of sweet expectation had become the day of bitter disappointment."

After the "dark night of disappointment," the Millerite movement, confused and divided in opinion, split into three groups. From one of these came the Seventh-day Adventist Church, a millenarian denomination which still survives as a viable faith, with a worldwide, growing membership.

William Miller died on December 20, 1849.

MORMONS.   See: *Orson Pratt; Brigham Young; Joseph Smith.*

A depiction of the angel Moroni delivering the plates of the
Book of Mormon to Joseph Smith, founder of the Church
of Jesus Christ of Latter-Day Saints, often called the "Mormon"
church.

Michel De Nostradamus (1503–1566). Perhaps the most famous prophet of all time, whose study of astrology culminated in the publication of his book, *Centuries*, a collection of rhymed prophecies many of which were exceedingly accurate.

"The Seventh Magic Figure" relates to the future of the Catholic Church and the Papacy made in a prophecy by Paracelsus.

Paracelsus (1493–1541). Physician, alchemist and mystic who made important contributions to the field of medicine as well as prophesying many events. He correctly predicted the time and place of his own death.

The oracle of Dodone was celebrated in antiquity. The
engraving shows the temple and, in foreground, the magic
tree that revealed the future. A chorus of Thebans dances
around it and, at right, priests prepare a victim for sacrifice.

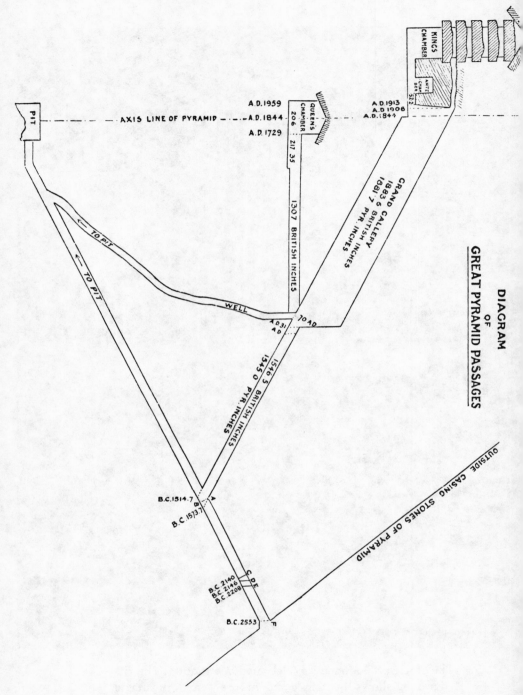

A diagram depicting the passages of the Great Pyramid at
Gizeh, one of the original seven wonders of the world. Though
it contains the so-called King's Chamber, there is no acceptable
evidence that a Pharaoh was ever interred there.

Girolamo Savonarola (1452–1498), a prophet who (as depicted here) made many of his prophecies in public, revealing his "divine" revelations before many large crowds. A Dominican monk, he was excommunicated and eventually martyred.

This illustration depicts characters from the plates of the Book of Mormon, which were used by discoverer Joseph Smith to found the Church of Jesus Christ Latter-Day Saints in 1830.

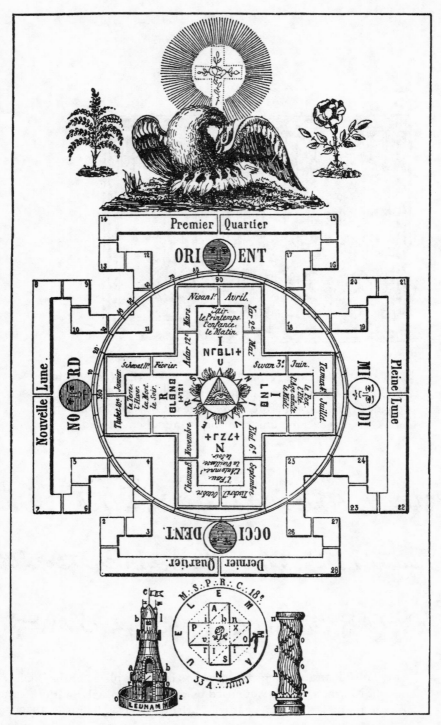

Mystical diagram of Solomon's Temple, as prophesied by Ezekiel and planned in the building scheme of the Knights Templar.

NIXON, ROBERT (The Cheshire Idiot) (b. circa. 1467).
A bucolic visionary who, according to popular belief,
was mentally retarded, hence the epithet associated with
his name. He was born on a farm near Vale Royale in
Cheshire county, England.

At an early age he was sent into the fields to plough,
his parents agreeing that he was too stupid to do any
other kind of work.

He was given to occasional monologues as he worked,
consisting of strange, dithyrambic utterances. His co-
workers paid little attention to these declamations, believing them to be merely the ramblings of an un-
sound mind.

One day, however, one of his more dramatic out-
bursts caught the attention of some of the other labor-
ers. The incident was to mark a turning point in his life
and to establish him as a gifted prophet.

"He was ploughing in a field," relates Charles

Mackay, "when he suddenly stopped from his labour, and with a wild look and strange gesture, exclaimed, '*Now, Dick! now Harry! O, ill done, Dick! O, well done, Harry! Harry has gained the day!*'

"His fellow labourers in the field did not know what to make of this rhapsody; but the next day cleared up the mystery. News was brought by a messenger in hot haste, that at the very instant when Nixon had thus ejaculated, Richard III had been slain at the battle of Bosworth, and Henry VII proclaimed king of England.

"It was not long before the fame of the new prophet reached the ears of the king, who expressed a wish to see and converse with him. A messenger was accordingly despatched to bring him to court; but long before he reached Cheshire, Nixon knew and dreaded the honours that awaited him. Indeed, it was said that at the very instant the king expressed the wish, Nixon was, by supernatural means, made acquainted with it, and that he ran about the town of Over in great distress of mind, calling out like a madman that Henry had sent for him and that he must go to court and be *clammed*—that is, starved to death.

"These expressions excited no little wonder; but on the third day the messenger arrived and carried him to court, leaving on the minds of the good people of Cheshire an impression that their prophet was one of the greatest ever born.

"On his arrival, King Henry appeared to be troubled exceedingly at the loss of a valuable diamond, and asked Nixon if he could inform him where it could be found. Henry had hidden the diamond himself, with a view to test the prophet's skill. Great, therefore, was his surprise when

Nixon answered him in the words of the old
proverb, 'Those who hide can find.' From that
time forth, the king implicitly believed that he
had the gift of prophecy, and ordered all his
words to be taken down."*

Among the events foretold by Nixon, which later
came true, were the civil wars in England; the way in
which King Charles II would die; the abdication of
James II of Scotland; the accession of William II of
Orange, the revolution, and the war with France.

Among those prophecies still to be fulfilled are these:
"Foreign nations shall invade England with snow
on their helmets, and shall bring plague, famine,
and murder in the skirts of their garments."

(Interpreters say this clearly forecasts an invasion
of Britain by the Russians.)

"The town of Nantwich a Cheshire village 45 miles
from Liverpool shall be swept away by a flood."

"Through our own money and our men,
Shall a dreadful war begin.
Between the sickle and the suck
All England shall have a pluck."

According to popular accounts, Nixon's prediction
of his own death by starvation came true—by a fluke.
In response to his frequent petitions to the king to allow
him to return home or that he would meet his death by
starvation, Henry gave strict orders to his officers and
cooks to give the prophet all the food he wished.

Eventually, however, while the king was absent, an
officer locked Nixon in the monarch's own closet to protect him from the mischief of palace servants, who

* Charles Mackay, *Extraordinary Popular Delusions and the Madness
of Crowds*. London, 1841.

envied him his special treatments. The officer was suddenly called away on a mission for the king, and forgot to leave the key for Nixon's release from the royal closet. When he returned, he found that the Cheshire Idiot had indeed starved to death, just as he had predicted he would do.

Occultists have theorized that Nixon was, from birth, possessed by a demon which had the Satanic powers of clairvoyance and precognition traditionally ascribed to them.

NOSTRADAMUS, MICHEL DE (1503–1566).   French physician, astrologer and the most famous prophet outside the biblical canon, was born at St. Remy in Provence on December 14, 1503. His parents were of Jewish origin, but apparently had been converted to Christianity. Some biographers have said that Nostradamus himself claimed to be of the tribe of Issachar, one of the ten lost tribes of Israel.

Nostradamus, who was a diligent student possessing an exceptional memory, was first tutored by his maternal grandfather, Jehan de Saint-Remy, an erudite physician. Later he studied the humanities at Avignon. Then he enrolled in the celebrated school of medicine at Montpelier, where he took the degree of Doctor of Medicine in 1529.

He practiced medicine at Agen, where he married, but later moved to Salon de Craux, near Aix-en-Provence. Two years after he had established himself there, a severe plague swept through that part of Europe, and his great skill as a physician was in much demand. He won considerable fame for his professional help in treating plague victims.

From his early youth, Nostradamus had been aware that he possessed to some degree "the gift of prophecy." He combined this natural talent with the art of astrology, in which he became increasingly absorbed. This study culminated in 1555 in the publication of *Centuries*, a book of rhymed prophecies that was destined to fascinate readers for centuries to come.

These predictions, consisting of 966 quatrains, are couched in an enigmatic, always vague, and sometimes incomprehensible language. They have no chronological order and in style resemble the sybilline oracles of ancient Greece, rather than the bold and forthright statements of Old Testament prophets, whose prophecies were also deeply religious and minatory in tone.

Some of the quatrains appear to be literal statements; others are symbolic. The idiom is a mixture of French and Latin, to which Nostradamus added a few neologisms of his own creation. Some names of people and places are given in the form of anagrams, e.g., Chiren for Henric (Henry II, King of France); and Ripas for Paris.

Nostradamus believed that only persons "inspired by divine power" could accurately predict future events. In the opening quatrains of *Centuries*, he describes the mood and setting for his work:

> *Seated at night in my secret study,*
> *Alone, reposing over the brass tripod,*
> *A slender flame leaps out of the solitude,*
> *Making me pronounce that which is not in vain.*
> *With divining rod in hand, I wet the limb and foot,*
> *Set in the middle of the branches.*
> *Fearsome awe trembles my hand, I await*
> *Heavenly Splendor! The Divine Genius sitteth by.*

Although Nostradamus wrote a number of treatises on other subjects, as well as another work of precognition called *Presages*, it was the *Centuries* which intrigued his contemporaries and has continued to be reprinted over the past 400 years.

When the first seven of the *Centuries* appeared in 1555, the book attracted the notice of Catherine de Medici, wife of Henry II of France, who invited the prophet to the Court in Paris. There he gained royal favor by his private readings for the royal couple and their three sons. In quatrain 35 of Century I, Nostradamus correctly predicted the King's odd manner of death.

Among the prophecies of Nostradamus which his interpreters say pertain to the present and the future are those which foretell the resurgence of the Arabs; a a warning to France not to join any military expedition to the Middle East; the restoration of Israel as a state; the coming of the Great Monarch, who will be born in Italy and will drive the enemies of Christianity from Europe, as well as the Russian alliance from Jerusalem; a time of calamities, lasting 27 years; the birth, reign and death of the Antichrist; the destruction of Paris; and the final war, culminating in the Last Judgment at about the year 2000.

Nostradamus predicted the time of his own death, which occurred at dawn on July 2, 1566. A marble tablet, inscribed in Latin, was erected over his grave. It reads:

> "Here lie the bones of the illustrious Michael Nostradamus, whose almost divine pen alone, in the judgment of all mortals, was worthy to record, under the influx of stars, the future events of the whole world. He lived 62 years, 6 months, 17 days. He died at Salon in the year 1566. Posterity, disturb not his sweet rest! Anne Ponce Germelle hopes for her husband true felicity."

ODILE, SAINT (c. 660–720).   Patroness of Alsace, was the daughter of Aldaric, the duke of Alsace. A 10th-century account of her life says that she was born blind, a fact which unaccountably angered her father, who had her taken secretly to a convent, to be reared by the nuns.

According to medieval sources, she miraculously received her sight when she was baptized by the bishop of Ratisbon. In commemoration of that event, portraits of St. Odile depict her holding a book upon which there are two eyes.

Because of her early blindness and miraculous gift of sight, St. Odile is considered the patroness of those suffering any disease of the eyes. Her feast day is December 13.

The prophecy attributed to St. Odile apparently predicted both world wars, and previsions the final chapter of human history in these words:

"Woe to those who, in those days, do not fear the

Antichrist; for he is the father of those who do not find crime repulsive. He will give rise to further murders, and many tears will be shed because of his evil ways. Men will set themselves one against the other; but at the end, they will want to re-establish order. Some will try to do this, but they will not succeed. They will be worse off than they were before.

"When things have reached a climax, and the hand of man can no longer do anything, affairs will be placed in the hands of Him who will send down a punishment more terrible than anything seen before.

"God has already sent the Flood, and he has promised never to send another. Instead, what He will do will be something unexpected and terrible.

"But the age of peace under steel will arrive; the two horns of the moon will become a cross. In those days, frightened men will truly adore God, and the sun will shine with unaccustomed splendor."

ORVAL, THE PROPHECY OF. Takes its name from an abbey which tradition says was founded in the 12th century by St. Bernard in the valley of Orval, Duchy of Luxembourg.

The abbey was destroyed during the French Revolution, but the abbot salvaged the monastery archives in which the ancient manuscript was preserved. Part of the prophecy alludes to the return of the Jews to their homeland; to the advent of the Son of Perdition; and to the time of the end:

"God alone is great; the blessings are given, the saints are about to suffer. The Man of Sin comes, born of mixed blood. The white flower becomes obscured during ten times six moons and six times twenty moons, then disappears never to appear again. Much evil, hardly any good in those days; many cities perish by fire. Come, then, Israel; return to Christ the Lord.

"The accursed sects and the faithful are separated into two distinct parts. But it is done; then God alone will be believed. The third part of Gaul and again the third part and a half will be without faith; as it will also be among other nations.

"And behold, already six times three moons and four times five moons, and all is separating and the *Time of the End* has begun.

"After a number not full of moons, God combats by His two Just ones, and the Man of Sin has the advantage. But it is done: the God of all, places a wall of fire before my understanding and I see no longer. May He be blessed forevermore. Amen."

PARACELUS, THEOPHRASTUS BOMBAST VON
HOHENHEIM (1493–1541). Physician, alchemist
and mystic, was born near Einsiedeln in the German
canton of Schwyz, Switzerland, on the 10th of November 1493. He was the only child of Dr. Wilhelm Bombast von Hohenheim, a nobleman and physician, who
tutored his precocious son in the natural sciences and in
medicine.

Very little is factually known about his youth, except
that he was admitted to the University of Basle when
he was sixteen; but after a brief period of study, he
relinquished his academic career to pursue his education with Johannes Trithemius, the abbot of Sponheim,
the most famous alchemist and mystic of his day.

After absorbing the teachings of Trithemius (or as
much of them as he could assimilate in a short time),
Paracelsus left the master to take up the study of metal-
lurgy under Sigmund Fugger von Schwatz in the mines
of Tyrol.

Always restless and eager in the pursuit of knowledge, he later became a medical student in Vienna, where he qualified as a physician. All his life thereafter, he was a ceaseless wanderer, seeking wisdom and inspiration, which he was convinced could not be found in books. His travels took him through Italy, Spain, Portugal, Germany, Poland, Russia, France, Scandinavia, Croatia, Turkey, and Greece.

Independent, outspoken, contemptuous of tradition and of the orthodox views of the medical profession, wherever he went, he quarreled with the authorities, gave inflamatory lectures, effected seemingly miraculous cures of the sick, and infuriated conservative elements of the community, who united in their determination—usually successful—to drive him out of their midst.

In 1526, owing to his reputation as a skilled physician and despite his revolutionary views, he was summoned to Basle to treat the famous publisher and humanist, Johannes Frobenius, who was on the point of having a gangrenous leg amputated.

Paracelsus was so successful in his treatment of Frobenius that his patient was up and about within two weeks, his leg all but restored.

The municipal council of Basle then appointed Paracelsus town physician, a position that carried with it a chair at Basle University.

It was not long, however, before he had alienated his colleagues and scandalized the town's medical establishment. He set the tone of his tenure at the university by circulating a printed leaflet announcing that he would lecture for two hours each day in German, rather than the academic Latin, on "practical and theoretical therapeutics, of which I myself am the author, with the highest diligence and to the great benefit of my listeners."

To emphasize his break with the past, he publicly burned the books of Galen and Avicenna, then standard works of reference. As he did so, he told other members of the faculty: "My beard knows more than you and your writers. My shoe buckles are more learned than Galen and Avicenna. Me! Me! I say you will follow—you, Avicenna, Galen, Rhazes, Montagna and Mesnes —I shall not be your follower, but you shall be mine."

Within two years, Paracelsus had taken his departure "in search of my art. . . I have not been ashamed to learn that which seemed to be useful from vagabonds, executioners and barbers. We knew that a lover will go a long way to meet the woman he adores; how much more will the lover of wisdom be tempted to go in search of his divine mistress."

His incessant wayfaring ended at last in Salzburg, where he died in 1541, having previously predicted the time and place of his demise.

Because of his important contributions to the field of medicine—in wound surgery, antisepsis, chemistry, even in psychosomatic therapy ("A powerful will may cure, where a doubt will end in failure")—Paracelsus is known chiefly as "the first great medical scientist."

But he was also a mystic, an adept in the occult arts, and a prophet. Eliphas Levi, the noted 19th-century Cabbalist, said of the prophetic work of Paracelsus that "it is the most astounding monument and indisputable proof of the reality and existence of the gift of natural prophecy."

Paracelsus presents his prophecies in the form of thirty-two "magical figures" or symbolic pictures, some of which recall the allegorical illustrations of the Tarot cards. Accompanying each figure is a prophetic text.

Like the *Centuries* of Nostradamus, the wording of Paracelsus's predictions is obscure, and there is no discernible chronology. Paracelsus says, somewhat mysteriously, that there are 32 figures in his series because "there are 32 symbols of that which is to be. May they not fly higher, so they but fall into the time for which they are intended."

He explains that in the figures, a city, a country, a government, or a kingdom is symbolized by the animals, arms or colors associated with those respective powers.

> "Therefore," he writes, "everyone who would undertake to interpret such prophecy should not only be a good astrologer, but also a good magus, and should know thoroughly what plant, animal or color each city, country, prince, or lord carries in the coat of arms."

For students puzzling over the magic figures more than four centuries after Paraclesus created them, this is indeed a tall order.

Paracelsus says he wrote the prophecies because "it it time to show men their madness, and it is this we propose to do by thirty-two figures intelligible but to a small number of the elect.

> "We have seen in the consummate iniquity of the people of Gomorha, carrying their blasphemies unto the heavens; but when things are pushed to extremes, the overbent bow breaks, and men are driven by a fatal law to a contrary extremity, whereby motion relaxes and the balance is established.
>
> "Thus by perpetrating crime after crime, corruption shall exhaust itself; and who can sadden thereat? Behold, the salvation of the multitude is coming, and redemption shall overcome the kingdom of evil.
>
> "The greatness of evil has not yet revealed itself.

It shall, however, reveal itself and with it a force shall become manifested that will prevent the just from being seduced and drawn into the ruin of the perverse."

The seventh magic figure of the Paracelsus prophecy (see illustration) relates to the future of the Catholic Church and the Papacy. The text which accompanies it reads:

"Because from time to time thou hast been self-willed, thou art predestined to be surrounded by much adversity. For thou hast not considered of thyself how thou art prefigured magically under the symbol of a stone, as both fat and lean. Thou dost not know it, therefore thou fallest beneath the punishment that hath broken up all empires. Had thy pretended wisdom and understanding been thine own, thou wouldst have been beyond disaster, and moreover, other empires would have taken thee as a mirror. But it is not so, therefore thy wisdom proveth to be a folly at this time."

PIUS X, ST. (1835–1914).   Pope, whose pontificate extended from August 4, 1903, to August 20, 1914. He was born Giuseppe Sarto, on June 2, 1835, the son of humble parents, at Riete, Italy.

Zealous in defense of the Catholic faith, he issued a condemnation of 65 propositions of Modernism. He was criticized in America for refusing a papal audience to Theodore Roosevelt because the former U.S. President was scheduled to speak in a Methodist church in Rome.

It is said that he had great personal charm, combined with deep personal humility and love for humanity. A dedicated pacifist, he was profoundly distressed at the outbreak of World War I, a development which hastened his death on August 20, 1914.

In 1909, during an audience for the general chapter of the Franciscan order, the Pontiff appeared to enter a trance state. Those present, somewhat taken aback, remained motionless and silent.

After a few moments, the Pope opened his eyes, rose from his seat and cried out:

> "What I have seen is terrifying! Will I be the one, or will it be my successor? What is certain is that the Pope will leave Rome and in leaving the Vatican, he will have to pass over the dead bodies of his priests!"

He then cautioned his audience: "Do not tell anyone this while I am alive."

Just prior to his death, Pius had another vision presaging the end of the papacy.

> "I have seen one of my successors, of the same name, who was fleeing over the bodies of his brethren. He will take refuge in some hiding place; but after a brief respite, he will die a cruel death.
>
> "Respect for God has disappeared from human hearts. They wish to efface even God's memory. This perversity is nothing less than the beginning of the last days of the world."

PRATT, ORSON. A prophet of the Church of Jesus Christ of Latter-Day Saints, who foresaw a major civil conflict in America, although he did not pinpoint a date for the event. In his *Journal of Discourses*, Vol. 20, he wrote:

> "What, then, will be the condition of the people when the great, dreadful war will come? It will

be very different from the war between the North and South. It will be neighborhood against neighborhood, city against city, town against town, state against state; and they will go forth destroying and being destroyed. Manufacturing will almost cease; great cities will be left desolate. The time will come when the great city of New York will be left without inhabitants."

PREMOL.   A monastery near Grenoble, France, where, in 1783, an ancient manuscript of prophecy was discovered among the papers of a notary who had been administrator of that religious house.

Authorship of the document—believed to date from the middle of the seventeenth century—is unknown. It has been surmised that it was written by an inspired monk, who was formerly resident in the monastery.

The prophecy describes periods of history as they pertain to France and to the Roman Catholic Church, from the time of the French Revolution up to the end of the world. It is believed that the seer used the term "years" to indicate centuries; and "hours" to mean years.

Among other things, the Premol prophecy predicts the annihilation of Israel; the invasion of France by enemy forces, who will destroy Paris by fire; the overthrow of the Vatican, and flight of the Pope; a major schism in the Church; a revolution in England; and the coming of the Grand Monarch forecast by many other visionaries.

The prophecy opens with these words:

"The spirit conducted me into the heavens and said to me: 'It is written that the Archangel Michael will do battle with the Dragon before the Triangle of God.'

"Then the spirit added: 'Open the doors of your understanding; the Archangel and the Dragon are the two spirits that will contend for the kingdom of Jerusalem; and the Triangle is the glory of the Almighty.' "

The Premol oracle presages the disintegration of the Catholic Church in a statement which seems very pertinent to today's events:

"And that is not yet all, O Lord! The Church has been destroyed by her own sons. The children of Zion are divided into two groups: one faithful to the fugitive Pontiff and the other in the service of the government of Zion, respecting the sceptre, but smashing the triple-tiered crown.

"And one places the mutilated tiara upon an ardent head, determined to institute reforms that the opposing faction rejects; and confusion reigns in the sanctuary."

The unknown monk, like other seers who came before and after him, foretells bloody conflicts on earth, marking the consummation of human history:

"Individuals and nations will rise against each other. Wars! Wars! Civil wars, foreign wars! What terrifying clashes! Everything is dead or in mourning; and famine stalks the earth.

"Must the elements also serve as an instrument of thy wrath? Stop, O Lord, stop! Thy cities are already crumbling by themselves.

"Pardon, pardon for Zion! But thou art deaf to our cries, and the mountain of Zion comes crumbling down with a deafening roar!

"The Cross of Christ now surmounts only a heap of ruins.

"And it is here that I see the king of Zion abandon

his staff and his triple crown and, shaking the dust of these ruins from his feet, make haste to flee toward other shores."

PREVORST, SEERESS OF (b. 1801).   Known only as Mrs. H., the seeress was born in the village of Wirtemberg, Germany in 1801. At an early age she became aware that she possessed the faculty of precognition, events of the future appearing to her in prophetic dreams.

From childhood, too, she experienced a hypersensitivity to metals and to dead bodies. She also reacted to what she described as magnetic influences of which those around her were not aware.

Her spiritual vision was heightened by gazing into soap bubbles, or mirrors, although she shrank from looking at either one. When she did so, she seemed to shudder and recoil, saying that she feared she might see something which would alarm her. On one occasion, when a child started blowing bubbles in her presence, she exclaimed: "Ah, my God! I see in the bubbles everything that comes into my mind, even though it is something distant—not in miniature, but as large as life. Still—it frightens me so."

Justinus Kerner, whose wife was an intimate friend of the seeress and who later wrote an account of her experiences, said that she was also a healer.

"When Mrs. H. looked into the right eye of a person, she saw, behind the reflected image of herself, another which appeared to be neither her own nor that of the person into whose eye she was looking. She believed it to be the picture of that person's inner self. In many persons, the image appeared to be more earnest than the external, or the reverse. It bespoke the character of the person; but with many it was more beautiful and pure than the other.

"If she looked into the left eye, she saw immediately whatever internal diseases existed—whether in the stomach, lungs, or elsewhere—and prescribed for it."

The seeress did not provide posterity with any long-range prophecies on the scale of Cayce or Jeane Dixon; but she did evolve a remarkably complex theory of psychic "sun spheres" and "life spheres," which she represented in a number of drawings.

The first of these diagrams, reports Kerner, "she called her sun sphere, or the solar orbit of her life; and she often repeated that everyone carries such a sphere of relative life around which she represented as his proper life sphere. This sun sphere is rather a series of spheres, drawn around one center. The successive spheres alternate in their properties, in the same manner as the alternate spheres of repulsion and attraction that surround the sun, and are commonly represented to the popular reader as the centrifugal and centripetal forces of that luminary. It is evidently this analogy that compelled Mrs. H. to symbolize her enunciations on this subject in language belonging to the sun, and other celestial bodies.

"The circumference of the best-marked of all these orbits seemed to come out from the pit of the stomach, to lead over the breast, and pass around close by the left side. This is a sphere of nearly ten inches in diameter, described around the ideal center of the sympathetic nervous system. It is an ideal globe, placed in the left-front-side, and including within it the heart, the roots of the lungs, part of the stomach and, in fine, the principal ganglionic plexuses of nerves.

"Outside this is a boundless sphere, like the outer-most sphere of repulsion of a sun. This boundless one is really the first; but that which has been just described is always called the first, or *great orbit*, by the Seeress. Within the latter are six other orbits, successively 2nd, 3rd, 4th, 5th, 6th.

"The first (or as she calls it, the 6th, inverting the order she afterwards follows) was accompanied at its circumference with a sensation that suggested the conception of something higher than nerve, which she calls nerve-spirit. The area of this first orbit was divided into twelve parts or segments and marked by a great many points on its periphery. In the outer half, i.e., that which lay outside the pit of the stomach and breast, seemed to lie the work-day world of man. She there felt the spirit (*Geist*) of all with whom she had acquaintance, but without their bodies or their names. Kerner, least of all, was sensible to her as a body; she saw him like a blue flame at a particular point of the orbit, moving perpetually in the sphere, accompanied by his wife a little farther off.

"This first orbit was to her like a wall, beyond which she could not move. Her consolation was that she could speak to man the better from that confinement. She felt fixed to a particular point in the sphere, without power to advance; but regularly at midday and midnight, she was pushed half a point forward, making one point in the twenty-four hours. The day seemed to impel or to shove her.

"In the outer orbit, over which seven stars seemed to shine, she was at ease and happy. She spoke to the world from there, and thought that Kerner alone heard her. In the second orbit, she found it cold and repulsive. She did not speak, but only swam hither and thither over it, and twice saw into it, but only what was too horrible to remember. Yet this orbit had the light of the moon to it. "She averred that these seven stars signify nothing else but the stars, and the cold orbit the veritable moon. 'These stars are the abodes of blessed ones of a lower grade.' The second cold orbit is the abode of such as grow (i.e., are in the process of growing) holy; but that only on the right side. "The third orbit is sun-clear, and its middle point far clearer. In it she seemed to peer, with other spirits, down into an impenetrable deep of clearness, which she expressed as the sun of grace. Here she spoke out into the world, as in the first; and still more than in the first, nobody seemed to hear her but Kerner. She was still more isolated from all but him. In its clearness, she saw her conductress (or protecting spirit) except in its too-bright midpoint, and from this orbit, the prescriptions appeared to proceed, she knew not how! This is the dream-ring. In it she saw an intermediate region, and a region for the spirits of beasts, the latter undermost—all clearer than our day, with a uniform clearness, without light and shadow.

"When she wished to penetrate the central orbits, she had to bethink herself of the month, day, hour, minute and second in which she was; and then, whilst reading them off, she seemed to ride into these three innermost orbits as on a straight sunbeam. In all these she could see both past and future, history and prophecy."*

* Justinus Kerner, *The Seeress of Prevorst*. London, 1847.

PYRAMID, THE GREAT. The idea that the Great Pyramid at Gizeh is a "prophecy in stone," containing a symbolic time-table of human history, has excited more interest in the popular mind than any other topic connected with Egyptology.

As the massive pyramid is devoid of inscriptions of any kind, inside or out, interpretation of its supposed prophecy is based upon a reading of its measurements and structural features.

> "Knowledge symbolized by the general proportions of the Great Pyramid," declared John Garnier, one of the theorists, "and by the lengths and dimensions of its interior passages and chambers, is so profound that it suggests a wisdom which is more than human, not merely on account of the knowledge itself, but on account of the remarkable way in which this knowledge is expressed by the relations of a few simple measurements."

The Great Pyramid is, in fact, quite different from the other pyramids of Egypt, so far as its internal features are concerned. It seems apparent that the two other pyramids in the Valley of the Kings were built in imitation of the first and larger one.

Moreover, as Garnier observed, the builders of the later ones had no knowledge of the secrets of the Great Pyramid's interior, nor of the principles upon which it was constructed.

The lesser pyramids contain no chambers nor passages in their interiors except the passages descending to the underground chambers in which the mummy of the dead Pharaoh was entombed. The builders apparently were ignorant of the ascending passages and chambers in the Great Pyramid, which were hermetically sealed off with such ingenious workmanship that their existence was later discovered only by accident.

The colossal edifice remains to this day the most prodigious work of human hands.

> "What architect of the present day," asked Marsham Adams, "would undertake to erect a building more than 400 feet high, full of chambers of the most elaborate description, which would never need repair for 6,000 years?"

The pyramid has a base line of 775 feet, a volume of 88,500,000 cubic feet of masonry, weighing a total of 6,840,000 tons. Each of the 2,300,000 huge stone blocks comprising the pile weighs an average of two and a half tons. The gigantic edifice covers an area of about thirteen acres.

As Paul Brunton observed in his work, *A Search in Secret Egypt*, the pyramid's position is not only a central meridian for Egypt, but also for the entire globe, as it stands exactly on the middle dividing line of the earth.

> "If a vertical line is drawn through it," wrote Brunton, "the land area lying to the east will be found equal to the land area lying to the west of the line. The meridian of the Great Pyramid is thus the natural zero longitude for the whole globe. Its position on the land surface of the earth is therefore *unique*. And in perfect keeping with that position, its four slanted sides front the four points of the compass."

Originally, the sides of the pyramid were covered with highly polished white limestone, the dazzling effect of which in the sunlight excited the admiration of the ancients, who regarded it as one of the seven wonders of the world. The casing blocks were stripped off about A.D. 900 by the Egyptian caliphs, who used them in construction of their own palaces.

The entrance to the pyramid is situated on the north face, 48 feet above the base line. From the entrance, a descending passage leads to an unfinished chamber 101½ feet below the plateau level.

At a distance of about 90 feet from the entrance, the first ascending passage (formerly completely hidden) commences. It continues for 130 feet and then opens into the Grand Gallery, which is 157 feet in length, seven feet in width, and 28 feet in height. These ample dimensions contrast sharply with those of the descending and ascending passages, each of which is three and a half feet wide and only four feet high.

At the upper end of the Grand Gallery is a low passage leading into a small room called the ante-chamber, and from there another low passage leading upward to the so-called King's Chamber. The latter is 34 feet long, 17 feet wide, and about 19 feet high.

Near the entrance of the Grand Gallery, another low passage branches off and running horizontally beneath it, leads into another room called the Queen's Chamber, the center of which lies exactly under the apex of the pyramid.

Esoterists, who hold that the Great Pyramid is a prophetic monument, claim that there is a chronological line running through the huge edifice, along which are indicated significant dates in human history. The unit of calculation on this scale is usually considered to be one inch equal to one year. (Some interpreters say that the unit of measure changes at the Great Step inside the Grand Gallery, from one inch to the year to one inch to the month. The distance from the step to the end of the King's Chamber is believed to be a dimension of events to take place "in these latter days.")

Calculations involve a complicated system of reckoning, starting from a point obtained by a geometrical construction based on the pyramid's architectural parameters.

The over-all calendar is thought to cover the entire Adamic age of 6,000 years, starting with the year 4,000 B.C. The prophetic computation is closely related to Hebrew and Christian religious history, with the messianic Jesus as the central figure of the entire prophecy.

The various passages and chambers are symbolically related to such historical events as the Exodus of the Israelites, the date of the Crucifixion, the Christian dispensation or "Times of the Gentiles," World War I, the Final Tribulation, the coming of the Grand Monarch, and the time of the end—September 2001.

Most academic archeologists, historians and Egyptologists view the prophecy theories of the Great Pyramid as mere superstition. Some historians have expressed the same opinion. H. G. Wells, with his characteristic arrogance, contemptuously referred to the Egyptian pyramids as "unmeaning sepulchral piles."

On the other hand, scholars of vastly greater knowledge of the subject are convinced that the Great Pyramid, at least, represents something more than an ancient tomb. There is, in fact, no acceptable evidence that a dead Pharaoh was ever interred there.

ROME IN PROPHECY. *"Coliseus stabit et Roma;
quando cadet Coliseus, cadet et Roma; quando cadet
Roma, cadet et mundus."* (As long as the Coliseum
stands, Rome will stand; when the Coliseum falls, Rome
will fall; when Rome falls, so also will the world.)

So wrote the Venerable Bede, a British monk of the
7th century. Rome, perhaps more than any other city
except Jerusalem, is pivotal in many prophecies concerned with last things.

The firm belief that the destruction of Rome will
mark the end of the world is based in part upon the
Apocalypse of John. In his prophecy, he wrote that
final judgment will come upon the City of the Seven
Hills "in a single day—pestilence, bereavement, famine,
and burning. . ."

> "The kings of the earth who committed fornica-
> tion with her and wallowed in her luxury will
> weep and wail over her, as they see the smoke of

her conflagration. They will stand at a distance,
for horror at her torment, and will say, 'Alas, alas
for the great city, the mighty city of Babylon! In
a single hour your doom has struck!
"The merchants of the earth also will weep and
mourn for her, because no one any longer buys
their cargoes—cargoes of gold and silver, jewels
and pearls, cloths of purple and scarlet, silks and
fine linens; all kinds of scented woods, ivories,
and every sort of things made of costly woods,
bronze, iron or marble. . .''

According to a prophecy by St. Benedict of Nuria
(c. 542), Rome will not be destroyed by invading armies, but by natural forces such as storms and earthquakes.

Brigit of Sweden (1302–1373), who resided in Rome
for many years, said that it was revealed to her in a
vision that "first the sword and then fire" would assail
Rome. Afterward, the plough would pass over the city's
ruins.

Interpreters of Nostradamus say that he predicts
that Rome will be invaded by an allied army of Arabs
and Asiatics. In *Centuries* II, 93, he foresees the destruction of Castel Sant'Angelo and the Vatican, with
the Pope being taken captive and an antipope being
seated in his place.

Other prophecies forecast the end of Rome by a sudden inundation which will result in the whole city being submerged.

RIBERA, FRANCISCO (1537–1591). A Jesuit scholar
and expositor, he was born in Villacastin, Spain, in
1537. He was educated at the University of Salamanca,
where he later taught.

During Ribera's lifetime, the Protestant exposition of

the Apocalypse, led by Luther's antipapal movement, related the prophecies concerning the Antichrist to the papacy. The force and influence of these interpretations came to be so widely accepted that they became a matter of serious concern to the Vatican.

To counter the Protestant application of the various prophetic symbols to the Roman hierarchy, Ribera set himself to the task of presenting a different and equally persuasive interpretation of the Biblical prophecy.

The result was a 500-page commentary on John's Apocalypse, in which the learned Jesuit repudiated the Protestant reading of the Scriptures and offered a new exegesis.

His exposition, known as the Futurist system, asserted that the prophecy concerning the Antichrist could not refer to the papacy, but rather to some future man of sin.

The Antichrist would reign for three and one-half years, during which time he would abolish Christianity, be accepted by the Jews, and set up his own religion in Jerusalem, from which city he would rule the world as a dictator.

While admitting that Babylon the Great "the mother of harlots and abominations of the earth" described in John's Apocalypse was indeed the Catholic Church, Ribera affirmed that it meant the Church as she existed in the age of the pagan emperors "and as she will be in the end of the world," when she will have fallen away from the faith.

In its essentials, Ribera's interpretation closely resembles that of today's Protestant fundamentalists.

RUSSIA IN PROPHECY.   One of the most prescient forecasts concerning Russia was not uttered by a seer,

but by that country's emperor, Peter the Great (1672–
1725). In his last will and testament, he declared:

> "I found Russia a rivulet; I shall leave it a river;
> and my successors will make of it a great ocean,
> destined to fecundate Europe, and its waters will
> overflow the whole continent, in spite of the dikes
> with which weak hands seek to restrain it, if my
> descendants understand how to direct its course."

Two hundred years after this prediction was made,
a British astrologer-visionary confirmed the prophecy.
In his *World Predictions*, published in 1925, Cheiro
wrote that "a new idea of government will, little by
little, spread from this country [Russia], which will
completely revolutionize Europe, Asia and the Far East,
and Russia will become the most dreaded power in the
history of modern civilization.

> "Even the Church will have revolution within it-
> self. Strange creeds will be preached from all pul-
> pits.
> "For a time, religion will save herself from catas-
> trophe by abolishing' her Bishops' palaces, her
> gilded ceremonies and her alliance with Mon-
> archs. State and church will separate and will
> cease backing up one another. Under the guise of
> humility, religion will creep back to her cradle
> of poverty and persecution, and in the next hun-
> dred years, there will be as many religious sects
> in the world as there are pieces of the supposed
> "true Cross" in existence at the present time."

With the United States and Russia—the world's two
superpowers—passing from one confrontation to an-

other on the international stage, it is not surprising that many contemporary seers and near-seers have predicted a terrible nuclear war between the two countries.

During the years between 1945 and 1954, a girl in Holland experienced numerous apparitions of the Virgin Mary, who identified herself as Our Lady of All Peoples and who, among other prophetic revelations, told the young visionary:

> "It is here that a great conflict will occur—America, Russia. . . the time is not far off.
> "The Lady extended her hands in a protective gesture over a region that seemed to me to be the Ukraine. And I saw an infernal fire raging above, to the left of me, in Russia. It appeared to me to be the result of a great explosion that erupted from the earth.
> "The Lady said: 'And so you see, nothing remains.' And I looked upon what was virtually a deserted plain."

Biblical expositors of the millenialist school have identified the U.S.S.R. as Magog of Ezekiel's prophecy, destined to lead the armies of a northern confederacy against Israel. Gog, a proper name, is believed to be the prophetic designation of a future Russian leader who will command the invaders from the north.

The prophecy is repeated in John's Apocalypse, in which the hosts of Gog and Magog are seen assaulting the city beloved by God—i.e., Jerusalem—only to perish amid the immense slaughter of Armageddon.

> "When the thousand years are over, Satan will be let loose from his dungeon; and he will come out to seduce the nations in the four quarters of the earth and to muster them for battle, yes, the hosts of Gog and Magog, countless as the sands of the

sea. So they marched over the breadth of the land and laid siege to the camp of God's people and the city that he loves. But fire came down on them from heaven and consumed them; and the Devil, their seducer, was flung into the lake of fire and sulphur, where the beast and the false prophet had been flung, there to be tormented day and night forever."

SAVONAROLA, GIROLAMO (1452–1498). Dominican monk, martyr, and prophet of the Italian
Renaissance, was born at Ferrara, Italy, on September
21, 1452. He was the third son of Michele Savonarola
and Elena Bonacossi. His grandfather, who was a distinguished scientist and man of letters, was physician
to the court of the Duke of Ferrara.

Girolamo, too, was intended for a medical career, but
in his early youth he turned instead to a study of St.
Thomas Aquinas and the Hebrew prophets. In 1475,
he entered the Dominican monastery at Bologna. In
a letter to his father, he explained why:

"The reason which moves me to enter the religious
life is this; first, the great misery of the world, the iniquities of men, the ravishing, the adultery, the pride,
the idolatry, the cruel blasphemies; for the age has
come to such a pass that not one is found who acts
rightly; wherefore, many times a day did I sing to myself this verse, with tears: *Heu! fuge crudeles terras,*

fuge litus avarum. (Woe! flee from the world of inhumanities; flee from the haunts of greed and lust.)"

As Savonarola plunged deeper into a study of the Old Testament prophets and the Apocalypse of John, there began to stir in him the prophetic impulse. He began to see visions and to hear voices; he became fired with the zeal of the reformer, convinced that God had given him the divine mission of preaching repentance and of forewarning the people of the calamities which would befall both the church authorities and lay society because of their evil ways.

"You are making me a prophet by force," he cried in one of his sermons. "The sins of Italy force open my mouth. An inward fire consumes my bones and compels me to speak."

So he began to speak publicly of his visions, saying that they were divine revelations. On the night of Good Friday in 1492, he had a vision of two crosses, one black (which he interpreted as symbolizing the wrath of God) and the other golden (representing the mercy of God, over Jerusalem.)

Later, after Alexander VI had succeeded to the chair of Peter in a papal election that was believed to be fraudulent, Savonarola announced that he had beheld in a vision a hand in the heavens holding a sword over Rome, in which the point was turned toward the earth.

As public enthusiasm for his prophetic sermons grew, his denunciations of Church prelates and state princes became bolder and more powerful. He warned the people of Brescia that the walls of their city would one day be bathed in torrents of blood. That prediction, like virtually all those made by the fiery prophet, came true when in 1500, the French forces overran Brescia in a terrible combat that resulted in a massive slaughter of the town's inhabitants.

Savonarola's sermon to the Florentines in 1494 foretold the invasion of Charles VIII, the French King, across the Alps, and declared that his coming was divinely ordained. The French did, indeed, enter Florence on November 17, 1494, and after a confrontation with the Florentine authorities, were persuaded by Savonarola to withdraw.

For a time, the patriot monk became in effect the dictator of Florence, even though he held no official political office. At his instance, many social reforms were undertaken, benefitting the people of the Tuscan city.

During the height of his influence, the notoriously pagan, pleasure-loving Florentines gave up their fine dress and jewels; sang hymns, and reared their children by the church's strict moral code. Many of them renounced the world and entered monastic orders.

In the carnival of 1497, Savonarola staged his famous "carnival of vanities" in Florence's main square, the Piazza della Signoria, where profane books, indecent pictures, carnival masks, etc., were cast into a huge bonfire.

Savonarola's impassioned sermons and prophecies of what the corrupt prelates of the Church and degenerate rulers of the state could expect as retribution from God, earned him the hatred of powerful adversaries, who plotted his downfall.

Pope Alexander VI, a Borgia, on the pretext that Savonarola had endangered the public peace with his inflammatory prophecies, was intriguing with the French, and refused papal orders to come to Rome, issued a bull of excommunication against him.

Undeterred, the rebellious friar declared the papal sentence null and void.

The pontiff then had him brought to trial as an imposter (because of his prophecies) and a heretic as well. On the basis of a false confession, obtained by torture, he and two of his followers were condemned to death. They were strangled, their bodies burned, and their ashes thrown into the river Arno.

Savonarola's final prophecy, made on the day of his death and carefully written down by his followers, was that Florence would suffer severe calamities during the reign of a future pope named Clement.

That prophecy, too, came true thirty-one years later.

SHIPTON, MOTHER (c. 1486–1561). Legendary English witch and soothsayer, known as the Yorkshire Sibyl, is supposed to have been born at Dropping Well, Knaresborough, Yorkshire, in about the year 1486. No biographical data concerning her is based upon trustworthy sources.

An early account of her life says that she was christened Janet Ursula by the abbot of Beverly. Her surname was reportedly Southill.

Her mother, Agatha, was reputed to be a witch, and neighbors, noting that Ursula was uncommonly ugly, called her "the Devil's child."

An 18th-century biographer described her personal appearance in these words: "Her stature was larger than common, her body crooked, her face frightful; but her understanding extraordinary."

An ancient Scottish chronicle reports that her entrance into the world was attended by "various wonderful presages."

"A raven croaked upon the chimney top; an extraordinary noise was heard about the house for several nights before; and a violent storm of thunder and rain was the immediate precursor of her arrival.

"It was also observed that as soon as she was born,

she fell a grinning and laughing, after a geering manner, and immediately the tempest ceased."

She is supposed to have married a builder named Tony Shipton in 1512, from whom she took the name by which she was known to posterity.

William Lilly, the famous 17th-century London astrologer, quoted eighteen of her rhymed prophecies in his *Collection of Prophecies*, published in 1654, saying that at that time sixteen of them had already been fulfilled.

Among other predictions, she is credited with having foretold the death of Cardinal Wolsey, and having foreseen the great fire of London in 1666.

Another curious prophecy attributed to her, seemed to prefigure the coming of the motor car, and development of radio:

> *Carriages without horses shall go,*
> *And accidents fill the world with woe.*
> *Around the earth, thoughts shall fly*
> *In the twinkling of an eye.*

It is said that Mother Shipton died at Clifton, Yorkshire, in 1561. For a number of years prior to 1839, a wax effigy of the Yorkshire Sibyl stood in Westminster Abbey, along with those of other noted persons, including Edward VI, Queen Elizabeth I, James I, and Oliver Cromwell.

SIGNS (of "the last days"). Various phenomena and events, which evangelical Christians believe will portend the imminent second advent and culmination of human history are:

— The "ingathering" of the Jews—that is, their return to Palestine and restoration of the state of Israel.

— The spread of atheism; schisms; rejection of the faith; the acceptance and practice of a false religion; spreading immorality.

— Rebuilding of the Third Temple in Jerusalem.

— The end of the papacy.

— Outpouring of the spirit upon the flesh. The Gospel of Christ will be extended over the face of the earth and will be made known to all people.

— Wars and rumors of wars. Great battles will be waged, resulting in inconceivable carnage.

— Prodigies and natural phenomena, and scientific wonders. These will include the darkening of the sun and moon; comets; space travel, and so on.

— Establishment of world government, with every citizen required to wear an identifying number or mark on his hand or forehead.

— Appearance of the Antichrist and persecution of the faithful.

— Beginning of a time of trouble and tribulation: earthquakes, floods, epidemics, famines, and economic depressions.

— Escalation of the Middle East crisis, leading eventually to Armageddon, the final, annihilating war.

SMITH, JOSEPH (1805–1844). Prophet and founder of the Church of Jesus Christ of Latter-day Saints, was born at Sharon, Vermont, on December 23, 1805. When Joseph was 10 years old, his parents moved to Palmyra, New York.

Several years later, he began to experience what he termed heavenly visions. When he was 22, he announced that, following angelic directions received in one of his visions, he had unearthed certain ancient scriptures, engraved on golden plates in characters that he defined as "reformed Egyptian." Using two optical instruments found with the plates, Smith translated the work and published it in 1830 as the *Book of Mormon.*

In that same year, Smith's new doctrine attracted a small group of followers, who organized the Church of Jesus Christ of Latter-day Saints, with Joseph Smith as their prophet and leader.

Guided by continuing visions and divine inspiration, Smith evolved the various details of organization and church canons, directing the growing membership in its many moves and struggles against the hostility of other denominations.

The persecution of the young church culminated in the murder of Joseph Smith and his brother Hyrum by a lynch mob in Carthage, Illinois. The murderers, who included members of the uniformed militia, stormed the jail where several leaders of the new faith, including its founder, were being held. The perpetrators of the crime were later brought to trial, but were acquitted.

The prophetic doctrine of Mormonism involves a belief in a second advent, with Jesus to rule from the New Zion, following his return to earth. The *Book of Mormon,* like the prophetic books of the Old and New Testament, predicts a time of calamities in the last days. 2 Nephi, 27, declares:

> "But behold, in the last days, or in the days of the Gentiles—yea, behold all the nations of the Gentiles and also the Jews, both those who shall come upon this land and those who shall come upon other lands, yea, even upon all lands of the earth, behold, they will be drunken with iniquity and all manner of abominations—

"And when that day shall come they shall be visited of the Lord of Hosts, with thunder and with earthquake, and with a great noise, and with storm, and with tempest, and with the flame of devouring fire."

SOUTHCOTT, JOANNA (1750–1814).   English prophetess, was born at Gittisham, Devonshire, in 1750. The daughter of a farmer, she had little formal education. She worked for a time as a domestic servant and later as a shop assistant.

When she was 42, Joanna began to write rhymed prophecies, which were widely circulated in Devonshire and London, even though they were somewhat obscure and at times even incomprehensible.

In 1802, she settled permanently in London, where she opened a chapel and attracted a number of followers, whom she began to "seal," thus making them a member of the 124,000 elect who would be gathered into heaven at the time of the end.

She was over sixty years of age when she announced that she would bear a divine child—Shiloh, the Prince of Peace—on October 19, 1814. This startling information was received with joy by her closest adherents, who prepared a cradle and clothing for the expected divine infant.

Joanna's detractors, however, accused her of having had intercourse with the Devil.

In reply, they were told that Satan was deprived of his creative power when he fell from heaven; if this were not so, the world long since would have become populated with his demonic offspring.

The date of the predicted birth passed uneventfully, and the prophetess died ten days later of a brain ailment.

She left a sealed, locked box with instructions that

it was to be opened at a future date in time of national crisis, but only in the presence of all 24 bishops of the Anglican church, assembled in one place. To date, the bishops have refused to consider her request.

A writer named Xenes reported a few years ago that he employed a clairvoyant to determine what the mystic box contains. He was informed that it was "a rough-looking box of deal or pine, similar to a seaman's chest, or perhaps such as was used in old times by domestic servants, and that it was corded about and sealed.

> "As to its contents, there was a complete layette for an infant, and in addition thereto a stole and cap very delicately worked and embroidered, a hood of crewel work, two separate batches of quarto-sized manuscript, and a bedspread of various colors. There was also a glass receptacle of some sort that appeared to be either a cup or a vase."

One prophetic couplet written by Joanne Southcott that could have application to the present day, reads:

> *When the Eastern war appears,*
> *Then know the end is near.*

SPENGLER, OSWALD (1880–1936).   German philosopher-historian and author, was born at Blankenburg, in the Harz mountains of Germany, on May 29, 1880.

Until the publication of his major work, *The Decline of the West*, in 1920–1922, which brought him worldwide recognition overnight, he was an obscure scholar. He was employed as a school teacher until 1910, but gave up that profession to pursue his major interest, the development of his theory that all civilizations pass through life-cycles like forms of organic life—that is, they grow from a primitive stage or youth, mature, grow old and die.

By a comparative study of the life-cycles of past civilizations, Spengler believed that the future of the present ones can be predicted. He could foretell "the spiritual forms, duration, rhythm, meaning and product" of Western civilization, which he found to be entering the autumn of its lifespan.

The Decline of the West is a monumental work of prophecy, as well as history, based partly upon intuition and partly upon an amazing, wide-ranging knowledge of mathematics, art, religion, and political systems.

Spengler predicts the decline and eventual eclipse of Western civilization, beginning with the period that followed World War I.

This decline, he says, will be a gradual one which will extend into the first centuries of the coming millenium. Looking beyond the apocalyptic date of 2000, which most inspired prophets believe marks the closing chapter of human history, Spengler envisions a decadent, almost soulless society, inhabiting "megalopolises"—immense cities "laid out for ten to twenty million inhabitants, spread over enormous areas of countryside, with buildings that will dwarf the biggest of today's, and notions of traffic and communication that we should regard as fantastic to the point of madness."

Future wars will be fought on a grand scale and "continents will be staked, India, China, Africa, Russia, Islam called out, new technics and tactics played and counter-played."

These wars, says Spengler, will be fought not by a draftee army, but by "volunteer, war-keen soldiers" whose numbers will no longer be in the millions, but hundreds of thousands.

> "These armies are not substitutes for war—they are *for* war, and they want war."

Spengler has a final word of advice for the lonely, fear-ridden "autumnal" man of a fading Western culture: have the courage to face the facts as they are.

"Let's choose *only* between victory and ruin—not between war and peace. And to victory belong the sacrifices of victory."

TENSKWATAWA ("Open Door"). Prophet of the
Shawnee tribe of American Indians, and twin brother
of Tecumseh. Little is known of the earlier and later
parts of his life. As a youth, he was given to drunken-
ness, self-assertion, and boasting. At that period of his
life, he was known as Laulewasikaw, or Loud Voice.

One day, as he was in the act of lighting his pipe, he
fell into a deep trance. His associates, believing him to
be dead, were preparing his funeral when he revived
and announcd that he had been in the spirit world
where he had received a communication from the
Great Spirit.

In keeping with Indian tradition, he now took a new
name—Tenskwatawa—and assumed the prophetic man-
tel of an aged Shawnee prophet named Penagashega
(The Change-of-Feather) who had recently died.

Taking his cue from the Christian missionaries, he
became a preaching prophet. He denounced witchcraft,
then prevalent among the Indians, "fire-water" and all
the white man's customs and institutions.

An impressive orator, he told his fellow Red men that he had gone up into the clouds in the spirit, where the first place he came to was the abode of the Devil. There he beheld all the Indians who had died drunkards, with flames issuing from their mouths.

His reputation as a prophet was greatly enhanced among his brethren when he accurately predicted an eclipse of the sun, which took place in the summer of 1806.

Thomas Jefferson, at the close of his term in the Presidency, wrote to John Adams, his predecessor in that office, concerning Tenskwatawa:

"The Wabash Prophet is more rogue than fool, if to be a rogue is not the greatest of all follies. He rose to notice while I was in the administration, and became, of course, a proper subject for me. The inquiry was made with diligence. His declared object was the reformation of his red brethren, and their return to the pristine manners of living. He pretended to be in constant communication with the Great Spirit; that he was instructed by Him to make known to the Indians that they were created by Him distinct from the whites of different natures, for different purposes, and placed under different circumstances, adapted to their nature and destinies; that they must return from all the ways of the whites to the habits and opinions of their forefathers; that they must not eat the flesh of hogs, of bullocks, of sheep, &c., the deer and the buffalo having been created for their food; they must not make bread of wheat, but of Indian corn; they must not wear linen nor woolen, but must dress like their fathers, in the skins and furs of animals; they must not drink ardent spirits; and I do not remember whether he exhausted his inhibitions to the gun and gunpowder, in favor of the bow and arrow.

"I concluded from all this that he was a visionary, enveloped in their antiquities, and vainly endeavoring to lead back his brethren to the fancied beatitudes of their golden age. I thought there was little danger of his making many proselytes from the habits and comforts they had learned from the whites, to the hardships and privations of savagism, and no great harm if he did. But his followers increased until the British thought him worth corrupting, and found him corruptible. I suppose his views were then changed; but his proceedings in consequence of them were after I left the administration, and are therefore unknown to me; nor have I ever been informed what were the particular acts of his part which produced an actual commencement of hostilities on ours. I have no doubt, however, that the subsequent proceedings are but a chapter apart, like that of Henry and Lord Liverpool, in the book of the Kings of England."

THOMAS OF ERCELDONNE (Thomas the Rhymer). Poet and prophet who holds an important place in the legendary history of Scotland. The year of his birth is not known; but he lived in the late 12th and early 13th centuries. His correct name was Thomas Lermont, and his seat of Erceldonne was near Melrose, Scotland.

During his visit to the castle of Dunbar, the Earl of March, knowing that Thomas had the gift of second sight, asked the seer what another day would bring forth.

Thomas, "fetching a heavy sigh from the bottom of his heart," is said to have replied in this vein:

"Alas for tomorrow, a day of calamity and misery! Before the twelfth hour shall be heard in Scotland, a blast which shall strike the nations with amazement shall confound those who hear it, shall humble what is lofty, and what is unbending shall level to the ground."

The Earl and his retinue waited anxiously the following day for the predicted calamity. When the ninth hour had passed without any sign of an unusual occurrence, they began to deride Thomas as a "driveller."

But as the Earl sat down to his midday meal, a messenger arrived to announce that the King was dead.

The prophecies of Thomas continued to circulate in Scotland for centuries after his death; and some attributed to him are still quoted in the highlands of his native land.

Thomas the Rhymer is known to students of English literature from an ancient ballad that tells of his seven years enchantment by a fairy queen.

URIM AND THUMMIM.   Literally, Lights and Perfections. Thought to refer to two gems of surpassing beauty and splendor, set in the breastplate of the high-priest of the ancient Israelites, and used for prophesying the future.

One scholar has advanced the theory that Urim and Thummim were two small images or teraphim deposited in the doubling of the breastplate, which answered in articulate voice the questions put to them by the high-priest. However, most scholars discount this idea because it smacks of heathen oracles and is contrary to the whole spirit of Hebrew religious practice.

Whatever the nature or substance of the Urim and Thummim, their use is plainly described in Scripture. This was to inquire of God and to receive a prophetic answer concerning important events.

According to Rabbinical tradition, the consultation was carried out in the following manner:

The high-priest attired himself in his robes of office

and entered the sanctum or holy place and stood before the veil that separated it from the inner sanctuary or holy of holies. In that position, standing upright and facing the Ark of the Covenant, he inquired in a low voice regarding the matter that was the subject of his petition. Then keeping his eyes upon his breastplate, he received, through the medium of Urim and Thummim, the answer to his query.

The person on whose behalf the inquiry was being made, stood behind him, but outside the sanctum.

Maimonides has stated that it was not lawful to conduct such an inquiry on behalf of individuals, but only for kings or religious dignitaries concerned with the affairs of their congregations.

VIRGIL (Publius Virgilius Maro) (70–19 B.C.). The famous Roman poet was born on October 15, 70 B.C. near Mantua, in the region north of the Po.

Virgil is supposed to have prophesied the future advent of Christ in his fourth *Ecologue*. During the Middle Ages, many legends flourished concerning the poet's knowledge of the occult arts. Dante in his great work *The Divine Comedy*, selects Virgil from among all the savants of antiquity to be his guide.

The prophecy believed to presage the birth of Jesus is contained in a congratulatory poem which Virgil addressed to his patron, Pollio, who was at the time Consul of Rome.

The verses concern the nativity of a child, whose birth would occur during Pollio's consulate, and whose remarkable endowments would confer great blessings upon mankind. He was to be of divine birth, to bring universal peace, and to command the respect of the whole world. He would destroy the serpent, but would bestow his blessing upon the brute creation.

Virgil cites as the source of his prophecy the Cumaean Sibyl.

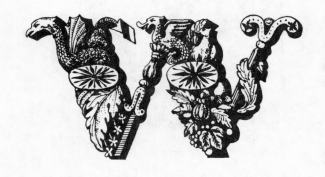

WOVOKA (19th century). Prophet of the Paiute tribe of American Indians, was the son of Tavibo, a Paiute chief and medicine man of Nevada.

Wovoka, claiming as did most other Indian prophets, that he had been taken into the spirit world, where the Great Spirit had revealed the future of the Indians to him, created a "Ghost-dance" religion. The latter spread rapidly until it embraced many tribes of the West and Midwestern United States. The prophet, who was known to whites as Jack Wilson, based the rites of his cult, which was known as the Big Moon, upon eating *peyote*.

"Peyote took pity on him," declared his nephew, George Anderson, "and guided him into the heavenly kingdom where, in a great vision, he saw signs and images representing events in the life of Christ; and was also shown the abode of the moon, the Sun, the Fire and the spirit forces tra-

ditionally regarded as the ancestors and elders
..."

In addition to revelations he received in peyote-in-
duced visions, Wovoka claimed that God also spoke to
him through the medium of an amulet he always wore
about his neck.

As other Indian prophets had done, Wovoka sought
to restore Indian moral and social values, which had
been eroded by their contact with the white man's civilization. He forbade the use of liquor; demanded fidelity
in marriage; and preached the emancipation of the Indians from the social customs of whites.

James Mooney, an authority on the Ghost Dance
Cult, reported that members of the Mormon sect who
encountered the Indian followers at the height of the
prophet's popularity, joined the cult, believing that the
Indians were descendants of one of the lost tribes of
Israel.

YOUNG, BRIGHAM (1801–1877). Mormon leader and prophet, was born at Whittingham, Vermont on June 1, 1801.

After the murder of the sect's founder-president, Joseph Smith in 1844, he assumed leadership of the young church. He organized and led the membership of some 5,000 persons from Illinois to the Great Salt Lake, Utah, where they established a settlement.

Young advocated plural marriage, and at the time of his death on August 29, 1877, was survived by 19 wives and 47 children.

In one of his prophetic discourses, he predicted both natural disasters and fratricidal wars in America during the twentieth century:

> "All that you now know can scarcely be called a preface to the sermon that will be preached with fire and sword, tempests, earthquakes, hail, rain, and fearful destruction. . . You will hear of

magnificent cities, now idolized by the people, sinking in the earth, entombing the inhabitants. The sea will heave itself beyond its bounds, engulfing many cities. Famine will spread over the nations, and nation will rise against nation, kingdom against kingdom, states against states, in our own country and in foreign lands."

ZECHARIAH (6th century B.C.). One of the Minor
Prophets of the Old Testament. The time and place of
his birth are unknown. He was a son of Berechiah,
and grandson of Iddo.

His prophetic ministry began after the return of the
Jews from their Babylonian exile, and extended from
the second to the fourth year of Darius Hytaspis.

The book of prophecies bearing his name falls into
two distinct divisions. The first is concerned with the
affairs of his own time, such as the rebuilding of the
Temple at Jerusalem, and the desire of the Jewish people to establish an independent, sovereign state.

The second section of his book, which is apocalyptic
in style and content, contains his visions of things to
come. Some of these prophecies have been interpreted
by reputable scholars to foretell:

— The coming of Christ and the blessings of his kingdom. (7:14)

— His triumphant entry into Jerusalem on an ass's colt. (9:9)

— His betrayal for 30 pieces of silver. (11:12)

— The stricken shepherd and his scattered flock, later referred to by Jesus himself. (13:7)

— The siege of Jerusalem (12:2, 14:2).

— The second advent. (14:3–21).